Cooking with

SUN-DRIED TOMATOES

Written by
Lois Dribin and Denise Marina

Illustrated by
Susan Ivankovich

FISHER
BOOKS

Publishers: Bill Fisher
               Helen Fisher
               Howard Fisher

Book Production: Paula Peterson
                    Nancy Taylor
Cover Design: Josh Young
Illustrations: Susan Ivankovich

Published by Fisher Books
PO Box 38040
Tucson, Arizona 85740-8040
602/292-9080

Copyright 1990 Fisher Books

Printed in U.S.A.
Printing • 10 9 8 7 6 5 4

**Library of Congress
Cataloging-in-Publication Data**

Dribin, Lois, 1947-
Cooking with sun-dried tomatoes/written
by Lois Dribin and Denise Marina;
illustrated by Susan Ivankovich.

p. cm.
Includes Index.
ISBN 1-55561-033-1: $9.95

1. Cookery (Tomatoes) 2. Dried tomatoes.
I. Marina, Denise, 1951- . II. Title.
TX803.Y6D75 1990
641.6'5642—dc20

90-13999
CIP

Notice: The information in this book is
true and complete to the best of our
knowledge. It is offered with no
guarantees on the part of the authors or
Fisher Books. Authors and publisher
disclaim all liability in connection with use
of this book.

Contents

This book is dedicated . . .

to my sweet, loving husband Richard.

Lois

to my husband Mike . . . my best support . . .
my dearest friend.

Susan

to my family; with special thanks to my grandmother, Adele,
for always being there.

Denise

Lois Dribin and Susan Ivankovich are the authors of the successful *Not-Strictly Vegetarian Cookbook*. For *Cooking with Sun-Dried Tomatoes*, they were joined by Denise Marina to feature this rediscovered cooking ingredient. All three live in the rolling hills of Bucks and Chester Counties near Philadelphia.

Introduction

Sun-dried tomatoes have captivated the culinary market. With their distinctive flavor and vibrant appearance, they have added a whole new dimension to the art of cooking. They enhance what seems to be an endless array of dishes from simple to elegant and lend themselves well to many culinary styles, especially those of the Mediterranean region.

We discovered sun-dried tomatoes on a cold wintry day several years ago while shopping at an Italian market in South Philadelphia. We saw a large glass jar filled with oil, garlic, herbs and red plum tomatoes. Upon inquiring, we were told they were sun-dried tomatoes. We were offered a sample. That was it! Sun-dried tomatoes made an indelible impression on our taste buds and on first encounter we became aficionados.

Inspired and with curiosity aroused, we began searching cookbooks for recipes featuring them. To our dismay we found they were rarely mentioned. Although they have begun appearing recently in recipes here and there and restaurants are now featuring them, there still seems to be a general lack of written information about them. However, nothing cooled our interest and enthusiasm. We began creating dishes highlighting this distinctive ingredient. To our delight we found sun-dried tomatoes complimented many of the foods we loved and we were thrilled with their versatility. We feel that they are here to stay and are taking their rightful place alongside the olive as a indispensable culinary staple.

Although a recent discovery for us, sun-dried tomatoes have long been a staple in the Mediterranean. There sun drying fruits and vegetables has been a necessary means of preserving food. Before the onset of modern technology, before the conveniences of refrigeration, freezers and modern ovens, our ancestors relied on the sun and fresh air to dry many of their foods. Dehydration allowed them to enjoy the fruits of their harvest throughout the year. Although we haven't the same concerns today, we still can appreciate the age-old method of sun drying. Through this process the brilliant color and robust flavor of the ripe tomato is preserved.

During the hot summer months, ripe plum tomatoes are picked at the peak of maturity. The luscious fruit is then sun-dried to a perfect texture, at which time it is generally packed in olive oil, often with the addition of herbs and spices. A certain alchemy takes place as the oil and herbs soften and flavor the tomato. In return, the essence of the tomato permeates and enhances the oil, rendering it almost as precious as the sun-dried tomato. Several companies here and abroad produce sun-dried tomatoes and the processes they employ vary. If desired, you can make sun-dried tomatoes at home and the results are delicious . . . quite honestly some of the best we've sampled. See pages 10—12 for more information.

Many of the recipes you'll find here have their roots in simple peasant cooking. Denise's spirited maternal grandmother Adele, has been a source of inspiration and folklore throughout many recipes in this book. Born at the turn of the century of French-Italian parentage, she was raised in a small

village by the Mediterranean Sea in Toulon, France.
Her recollections and memories of customs, cooking
and preserving have given us a heightened awareness
of the earthy simplicity of her time. There was a strong
reliance and respect toward the earth for nourishment
and sustenance.

She shared with us a late-summer tradition that
her mother ritually performed as soon as their garden
tomatoes were ripe. The small cherry tomatoes still
clinging to their vines were hung in a cool, dry
cellar along with the braided garlic, onions and
dried peppers.

The classic plum tomatoes which make such
wonderful sauce were gathered from the garden,
sliced in half and sun-dried to a firm consistency. This
is an early rendition of sun-dried tomatoes as we now
know them. The second harvest of plum tomatoes
was simmered into a sweet, concentrated paste that
was drained in fine netting for several days and then
placed on a wooden board to dry in the summer sun.
It was then spooned into an olive-oil-coated crock
and topped with a thin layer of olive oil that preserved
it throughout the year. This paste, diluted with either
wine or water, was used as a base for sauces and
soups. In this manner the delicious taste of fresh
tomato remained available throughout the winter.

Our culinary style is dictated only by our
imagination and our instincts. More often than not
our best creations come from sudden inspiration . . .
the discovery of a new ingredient, fresh herbs,
unusual cheese or an exotic spice can move us to
create an entire meal . . . such was our reaction when
we discovered sun-dried tomatoes. We hope our

enthusiasm is contagious and that this book will
arouse your creative interest.

Although eating is one of life's greatest pleasures,
it must be tempered with a sense of balance. Food
simply and lovingly prepared is what great cooking
and pleasurable dining means to us.

Making Sun-dried Tomatoes at Home

If you have the good fortune of an abundance of plum tomatoes either from your garden or a basketful from a local farmer's market, we urge you to consider making sun-dried tomatoes at home. You will be well rewarded as it takes little time, is quite simple to do and the results are some of the finest sun-dried tomatoes we've tasted.

Before going into the details of making them at home, we want to mention that the sun-dried tomatoes sold commercially most likely have not been dried in the sun. Although the Mediterranean enjoys a climate conducive to sun and air drying, it is unlikely that drying such large quantities of tomatoes would be practical.

Employing the sun for drying our own tomatoes naturally had great appeal. However, considering our weather conditions during the humid summer months in Pennsylvania, we knew the tomatoes would not dry quickly enough, thus encouraging mold to develop. We considered using either an electric food dehydrator or oven to do our drying. Electric food dehydrators can be purchased at a reasonable price and do a good job of drying a wide variety of fruits and vegetables. We decided, however, to use our ovens.

If you live in a hot, sunny, dry climate, by all means try sun drying. Be aware though that it takes several days for the tomatoes to dry sufficiently. You must provide protection from insects and birds. Cheesecloth, screens or insect netting works quite well for this. The tomatoes must be brought inside every evening before dusk to avoid the settling dew and returned to the sun the following morning.

This is how we went about it. We grew San Marzano plum tomatoes in our gardens. They are an excellent plum tomato, thick fleshed with few seeds. They are ideal for drying as well as making sauce. If you cannot find the Marzanos, other plum tomatoes do quite well. However, we do not recommend using any tomato other than plum because the liquid and seed content is too high. If you buy plum tomatoes, choose ripe fruit that is uniformly red.

Remove the stems of the tomatoes and rinse under cold water. Drain in a colander several minutes. Cut tomatoes in half lengthwise and with a spoon remove the seeds leaving the thick walls and skin intact. Place the tomato halves on top of a broiling pan, arranging the larger ones on the outer edge for more consistent drying. You may crowd the tomatoes close together. As drying begins, they will shrink. If you want all of your dried tomatoes to have the same texture and consistency, remove the smaller ones during the drying process because they take less time to dry. We've found that we enjoy both the slightly plump and leathery texture alike.

Cookie sheets are not recommended for this use. Another alternative is to wrap several layers of cheesecloth around the oven racks, placing the tomato halves on top.

If desired, before placing the tomatoes in the oven, sprinkle lightly with salt. It is not necessary to salt, but if you do, use it sparingly so the dried tomatoes remain naturally sweet and not salty. Place the tomatoes in the oven. Set the oven on warm or approximately 200F. Different ovens vary in temperature accuracy so expect to experiment a little. Close the door and let them dry overnight or 8 to 12 hours. Check after 6 hours; remove smaller tomatoes that have dried. It is not necessary to turn the tomatoes during the drying process. Four pounds of fresh plum tomatoes will yield approximately one pound of dried.

When they have finished drying, remove them from the oven and pack dried tomatoes into 1/2 pint jars. Cover with a good quality olive oil. We add a few cloves of garlic, a little fresh oregano and fresh thyme. You do not have to add herbs, but we found the garlic and herbs add a delightful flavor. We don't recommend using fresh or dried basil leaves. We were told that basil can turn the tomatoes bitter. If you have more than one or two jars you may choose to process in a hot-water bath or a pressure cooker, following manufacturers instructions. If not, place a tight-fitting lid on the jars and refrigerate. Allow the tomato and herb flavors to blend for several days before opening the jar. They will keep refrigerated for months.

Do not attempt to use your microwave oven for drying tomatoes. The microwave oven does not allow the moisture to escape, resulting in either burned or cooked tomatoes rather than dried. The results are unacceptable.

Things to Know About
Sun-dried Tomatoes

If you are familiar with sun-dried tomatoes, you've noticed that not all sun-dried tomatoes are created equal. Many companies are marketing them both here and abroad. They vary in quality and price. They also vary in taste, ranging from sweet to salty, seasoned in olive oil and with or without herbs. We prefer tomatoes seasoned in olive oil and lightly salted.

Once sun-dried tomatoes were found only in gourmet or specialty shops, but now they are available in supermarkets. Usually those bottled in oil will be in the specialty-foods area, while the dry-pack variety are in the produce section. Sun-dried tomato paste and tomato bits are also available.

A word of caution when using commercial dry-pack tomatoes in our recipes. Because they are extremely dry it is necessary to blanch them in boiling water about 30 seconds and drain well before packing in jars with olive oil and herbs.

You may want to alter our recipes according to the size of the sun-dried tomatoes you are using. If your tomatoes are small add a few more. Make adjustments accordingly, adding or decreasing the amount called for.

Appetizers

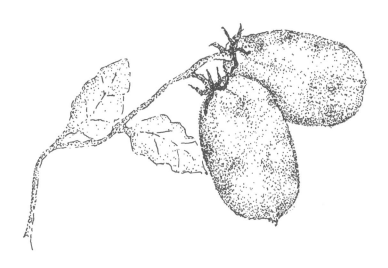

Denise has an unabashed passion for artichokes. Her relatives have been seen devouring this exotic-looking vegetable raw, the tender base of the leaves dipped in a little olive oil and salt. Here is a family recipe, redolent with garlic and Parmesan cheese, that is sure to soothe the savage soul or at least keep wandering vampires at bay.

Serves 4

Stuffing mixture:
1 cup unseasoned bread crumbs
1/2 cup freshly grated Parmesan cheese
2 garlic cloves, minced
2 sun-dried tomatoes, minced
1/2 teaspoon herb salt
Pinch of freshly ground pepper

4 medium artichokes
1/4 cup olive oil
3 whole garlic cloves

Combine stuffing mixture and set aside. Rinse artichokes and trim stems. With sharp knife, cut about 2 inches off tapered tops. With scissors, cut off sharp points of individual leaves. Spread the leaves open and stuff each opening with stuffing mixture. In a large pot heat olive oil and sauté whole garlic cloves until golden in color. Do not brown. Place artichokes upright in pan. Add water, covering all but the top quarter of the artichokes. Cover and simmer 45 minutes. After 30 minutes, baste artichokes with liquid they have been simmering in, making sure to moisten tops. Serve hot or at room temperature.

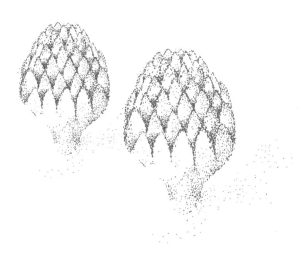

18 Mascarpone Cheese and Sun-dried Tomato Sandwich

Cut in small slices, this sandwich makes a lovely appetizer. We used a mascarpone cheese that was rolled with pesto. However if you can't locate this particular mascarpone, you can substitute a plain mascarpone or mozzarella cheese.

Serves 4 to 6

1 large thin French baguette
1/4 lb. mascarpone cheese
6 sun-dried tomatoes, cut into strips
1 small jar sweet roasted peppers
1 small bunch arugula
1 tablespoon olive oil
1 tablespoon wine or Balsamic vinegar

Preheat oven to 250F (120C). Cut bread in half
lengthwise. Spread cheese evenly over cut side of the
bread. Place sun-dried tomatoes on top of the cheese,
then peppers and arugula. Drizzle olive oil and vinegar
on cut side of other half of the bread. Close the loaf and
wrap in aluminum foil. Place in oven and heat 15
minutes. Remove from foil, cut into 1-inch pieces and
serve warm.

Chilled Vegetable Platter with Buffalo Mozzarella

Serve as an appetizer on a warm summer's eve.

Serves 6 to 8

1 medium eggplant, peeled and cubed
1 medium zucchini, cubed
1 red bell pepper, sliced into strips
1 red onion, sliced into rounds
3 large Portobello or domestic
   mushrooms
1 head radicchio, coarsely chopped
1/2 cup olive oil
4 large garlic cloves, minced
6 fresh basil leaves
3 tablespoons Balsamic vinegar
8 sun-dried tomato slices
12 Ligurian olives or other strongly
   flavored olives
Salt and pepper to taste
Red pepper flakes, optional
1 lb. Buffalo or other mozzarella,
   sliced

Prepare vegetables and place in a large bowl. Add olive oil, garlic and basil leaves. Mix well and let sit 1 hour, stirring occasionally. Spoon vegetables onto a large broiling pan and place under broiler 30 minutes, stir and mix every 5 minutes to prevent burning. Remove from heat and return cooked vegetables to bowl. Add vinegar, sun-dried tomatoes, olives, salt and pepper. Mix well, sprinkle with red pepper flakes if desired and chill 1 to 2 hours. Serve with sliced mozzarella on the side.

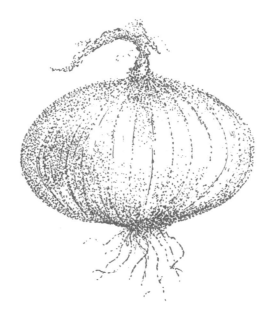

A modern version of a classic . . . Roman garlic bread with sun-dried tomatoes.

Serves 4

1 large crusty loaf Italian bread
1/4 cup extra-virgin olive oil
4 large garlic cloves, pressed
4 sun-dried tomatoes, finely chopped

Cut bread in half lengthwise, open it as wide and flat as possible. In a small bowl place olive oil, garlic and sun-dried tomatoes. Mix well and spoon evenly over bread. Place cut side up on broiler pan. Broil until golden, watching carefully to prevent burning. Slice bread and serve in a napkin-lined basket. Cover with another napkin to keep warm.

Biting into grape leaves and tasting bits of sun-dried tomatoes has definitely elevated these delicacies to new heights.

Serves a crowd

**1 (16-oz.) jar grape leaves packed
   in brine**
2 cups cooked rice
Juice of 1 lemon
2 tablespoons olive oil
1 small garlic clove, pressed
12 sun-dried tomatoes, finely chopped
4 tablespoons chopped parsley
1/2 cup pine nuts
1/4 lb. feta cheese, crumbled

Remove grape leaves from brine and rinse well to remove excess salt. Place grape leaves in a bowl and cover with water. Set aside. In another bowl, mix rice with lemon juice, olive oil, garlic, sun-dried tomatoes, parsley, pine nuts and feta cheese. Drain grape leaves and lay out one at a time. Put a heaping tablespoon of filling in a corner and roll up, folding in the sides as you roll holding the filling in. Repeat this process until you have used all of the filling. Refrigerate 2 to 3 hours. Serve chilled or at room temperature.

This is our improvisation of Anchoiade, an old classic from Provence. While Anchoiade is made predominately of anchovies, we have substituted sun-dried tomatoes. Serve this excellent spread as an appetizer on slices of French bread.

Serves 8 to 12

12 sun-dried tomatoes
6 garlic cloves
1 small bunch flat-leaf parsley
1/2 teaspoon anchovy paste,
  optional
1/4 cup freshly grated locatelli or
  Parmesan cheese
1/4 cup olive oil
1 tablespoon Balsamic vinegar
2 to 3 thin French baguettes

Place sun-dried tomatoes, garlic, parsley, anchovy paste if desired, locatelli or Parmesan, olive oil and vinegar in a food processor or blender and blend to a coarse paste. Cut bread in 1-inch slices and spread 1/2 to 1 teaspoon of the mixture evenly over top of each slice. Place on a cookie sheet and put under broiler 3 minutes checking every minute to prevent overcooking. Serve warm.

W*hat a great combo!*

Serves 4

1 lb. asparagus spears
1/2 cup water

Dressing:
6 sun-dried tomatoes,
**   chopped**
1/4 cup olive oil
1/8 cup Balsamic vinegar
1 garlic clove, pressed
Salt and pepper to taste

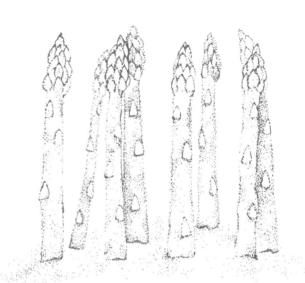

Red leaf lettuce

Wash and trim asparagus, place in skillet. Add water, cover and steam 8 minutes. Do not overcook, spears should be tender crisp and bright green. Drain off excess water and set aside to cool.

To Make Dressing: place sun-dried tomatoes in a small bowl and add olive oil, vinegar, garlic, salt and pepper. Mix thoroughly. Place asparagus on a flat dish and pour dressing on top. Cover and refrigerate several hours or overnight.

Serve on a generous portion of red leaf lettuce, spooning some of the dressing on top.

*C*aponata can be served as a side dish, a spread on thin slices of Crostini or an appetizer. It also makes an inspired open-face sandwich with melted mozzarella and arugula.

Serves 4

2 Japanese eggplants or 1 medium
    eggplant, cut into 1-inch cubes
Salt
1/4-1/2 cup vegetable oil
2 tablespoons virgin olive oil
1 small white onion, finely chopped
3 garlic cloves, finely chopped
3 sun-dried tomatoes, finely chopped
1 cup pitted green olives,
    coarsely chopped
1 tablespoon capers
Salt to taste
1 tablespoon sugar
1/2 cup Balsamic vinegar

Sprinkle eggplant cubes with salt and drain in a colander 1/2 hour. Press gently with a wooden spoon to remove any liquid. Heat vegetable oil in a large skillet and fry eggplant cubes, adding more oil if needed. Drain eggplant on paper towels. Discard vegetable oil you used for frying and wipe skillet with a paper towel. Add 2 tablespoons olive oil and sauté onion, garlic, sun-dried tomatoes, olives, capers and salt several minutes. Add eggplant, sugar and vinegar. Simmer 5 minutes. Cool to room temperature and serve. Refrigerated, caponata lasts a week.

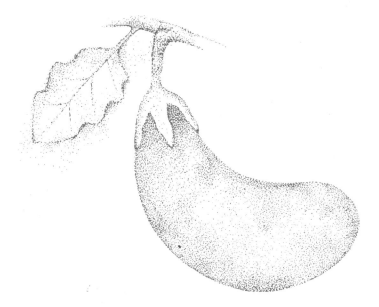

ᔰ *Crostini is good-quality Italian bread or French baguette cut in thin slices and toasted lightly. It can be topped with a spread or lightly brushed with garlic and olive oil.*

Serve this colorful dip as an appetizer, spread on thin slices of crusty French bread or with a platter of crudités. The zesty flavor will keep guests coming back for more.

Makes about 1 cup

7 to 10 sun-dried tomatoes
2 (3-oz.) pkgs. cream cheese,
   softened
2 to 3 garlic cloves
1 tablespoon oil from sun-dried
   tomatoes

Place all ingredients in a blender or food processor and blend together for 1 minute. Place in an attractive serving bowl; cover and refrigerate until ready to serve.

Salads & Soups

*F*estive and flavorful, this pasta salad is perfect picnic fare.

Serves 3 to 4

Salad:
1 lb. tri-color fusilli or other pasta
3/4 lb. Boucheron or feta cheese,
    crumbled
1/4 cup red onion, minced
1/2 cup sun-dried tomatoes, diced
1 cup Picholine or other green olives,
    pitted
1/2 cup chopped marinated
    artichoke hearts
1 cup coarsely chopped fresh
    sorrel leaves

Dressing:
1 garlic clove, minced
1/2 teaspoon herb salt
1/4 teaspoon freshly ground pepper
1/4 cup Balsamic vinegar
1/2 cup extra-virgin olive oil

Cook fusilli as directed. Drain and transfer to a mixing bowl. Add cheese, onion, sun-dried tomatoes, olives, artichoke hearts and sorrel leaves.

To Make Dressing: combine garlic, herb salt, pepper, vinegar and olive oil in a cruet with lid and shake well.

Pour dressing over the salad and mix lightly with wooden spoon. Serve at room temperature.

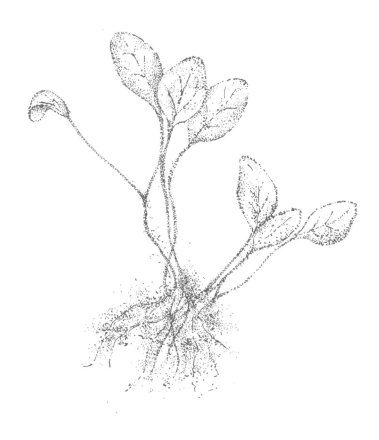

The simplicity of this salad demands the freshest ingredients . . . only summer-ripe tomatoes, fresh basil and parsley will do!

Serves 4

**5 firm ripe tomatoes, cut into 1/4-inch
    slices**
1/2 lb. mild mozzarella, sliced thin
**3 sun-dried tomatoes, cut into
    thin strips**
**1 medium Vidalia or sweet yellow
    (Spanish) onion, cut into thin rounds**
6 fresh basil leaves
3-4 flat-leaf parsley sprigs
1/4 cup extra-virgin olive oil
Salt and freshly ground pepper to taste

Arrange tomatoes, circular fashion, on a large,
flat serving dish (they may overlap one another).
Alternate mozzarella slices atop the tomato slices
creating a pinwheel design. Place sun-dried tomato
strips on top of the mozzarella. Top with onion slices.
Garnish along the outside rim of the plate with basil
and parsley, placing a basil leaf nosegay in the center.
Drizzle with olive oil and let sit at room temperature
15 or 20 minutes to marinate. Just before serving,
sprinkle with salt and pepper and enjoy this luscious
summer treat!

*A*n elegant pasta salad that takes only minutes to prepare.

Serves 4

**1 lb. cheese tortellini or plain and/or
  spinach tortellini
6 sun-dried tomatoes, chopped
6 sweet roasted peppers, chopped
12 black olives, pitted
2 oz. marinated goat cheese, crumbled
3 tablespoons extra-virgin olive oil
5 tablespoons Balsamic vinegar
2 tablespoons oil from sun-dried
  tomato jar
1 small flat-leaf parsley sprig, chopped
7 fresh basil leaves, chopped
Salt and pepper to taste**

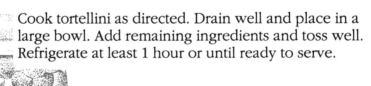

Cook tortellini as directed. Drain well and place in a large bowl. Add remaining ingredients and toss well. Refrigerate at least 1 hour or until ready to serve.

Three unique flavors topped with a simple dressing of olive oil and a little lemon. A visual compliment to any table.

Serves 2 to 4

1 medium fennel bulb
12 green and/or black Greek olives
3 sun-dried tomatoes, finely chopped
2 sprigs fresh flat-leaf parsley,
   finely chopped
3 teaspoons extra-virgin olive oil
Juice of 1 lemon
Salt and pepper to taste

Remove the top from the fennel and slice the bulb in very thin circles. Place in a colander and rinse thoroughly with cold water. Drain well. Place fennel in a large bowl, add olives, sun-dried tomatoes and parsley. Sprinkle with olive oil and lemon juice. Add salt and pepper to taste. Toss well and serve.

Chickpea (Garbanzo Bean)
and Olive Salad

This salad is enlivened with the fresh flavors of garlic, sun-dried tomatoes and herbs. Prepare a day or two in advance as the flavor intensifies with marinating. Serve as an appetizer or a side dish with roasted chicken.

Serves 4 or 5

**1-1/2 cups dried chickpeas
(garbanzo beans)**
1/2 cup extra-virgin olive oil
3 tablespoons Balsamic vinegar
4 large garlic cloves, minced
1/2 teaspoon salt
Pepper to taste
1/4 teaspoon finely chopped rosemary
**1 teaspoon finely chopped
flat-leaf parsley**
**1/4 teaspoon finely chopped fresh
tarragon, optional**
**1/2 cup Picholine or other green olives,
pitted**
1/4 cup Ligurian black olives, pitted
3 sun-dried tomatoes, finely chopped
1 medium onion, minced

Rinse chickpeas (garbanzo beans), place them in a
medium bowl and cover with water. Soak overnight.
Place chickpeas in a medium saucepan with soaking
liquid. Bring to a boil over high heat. Reduce heat and
simmer 1-1/2 to 2 hours until chickpeas are tender. In
a small bowl, whisk together olive oil, vinegar, garlic,
salt, pepper and fresh herbs. Drain chickpeas. In a
medium shallow bowl combine chickpeas, olives,
sun-dried tomatoes and onions. Pour olive-oil mixture
over top and mix together. This salad is best if it is
allowed to marinate overnight.

*T*his salad combines some of our favorite salad greens.
*The varying colors, tastes and textures naturally compliment
one another.*

Serves 2 to 4

1 small head radicchio
1 head Bibb lettuce
1 head mache (lamb's lettuce)
1 small bunch arugula
1 small red onion, cut into rings
1/4 cup virgin olive oil
2 tablespoons Balsamic vinegar
2 sun-dried tomatoes, mashed
  into a paste
1/4 cup pine nuts
Salt and ground pepper to taste
1/3 cup crumbled goat cheese

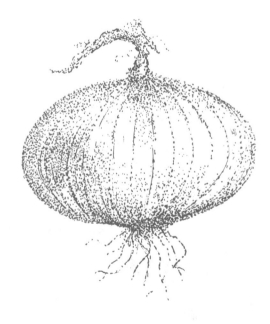

Tear apart radicchio and Bibb leaves to separate. Trim
and core mache or leave whole if desired. Tear arugula
in bite-sized pieces. Rinse all greens well and either roll
in towel or place in a salad spinner to dry. Place greens
and onion in a bowl; set aside. Whisk oil, vinegar and
sun-dried tomato paste together in a small bowl. Toast
pine nuts in a small skillet over low heat until golden.
Set aside. Sprinkle salt and pepper directly over the
greens. Pour just enough salad dressing over greens to
moisten. Add crumbled cheese and top with toasted
pine nuts. Toss and serve immediately.

*Radicchio is the size of Bibb lettuce and adds color
and a subtle bite. Bibb is mild with a buttery flavor.
Mache has a delicate, flowery touch and arugula,
an intense taste, almost spicy. Denise's 82-year-old
grandmother Adele enjoyed arugula as a young girl
in Toulon, France. It grew wild in the fields and was
a favorite among the villagers.*

This salad appeals to the peasant in us. Some of the simplest meals are the most satisfying.

Serves 4

1/2 loaf day-old French or Italian bread

2 large ripe tomatoes, cut into 1/2-inch pieces

2 sun-dried tomatoes, cut into small pieces

1 tablespoon capers

1/4 cup chopped, pitted Picholine olives or pitted green olives

1/2 cup extra-virgin olive oil

1/4 cup red wine vinegar

Salt and freshly ground pepper to taste

2 cucumbers, peeled, cut into 1/2-inch slices

1 small red onion, peeled, thinly sliced into rings

1 small bunch arugula for garnish

Slice bread in 1/2-inch thick slices. Set aside. Mix
tomatoes, sun-dried tomatoes, capers and olives
together in a bowl. Add olive oil, vinegar, salt and
pepper. Set aside. Place a layer of bread slices in a
wide shallow bowl. Arrange 1/2 the cucumbers and
onions over bread. Spoon 1/2 the tomato mixture
over bread and vegetables. Add another layer of bread
slices, cucumbers and onion, ending with tomato
mixture. Refrigerate about 1 hour. Allow to sit at room
temperature 5 to 10 minutes before serving. Garnish
by surrounding mixture with arugula leaves.

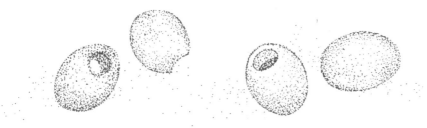

A hearty and satisfying meal in itself. Serve with a tossed green salad and a loaf of crusty bread.

Serves 6 to 8

1/4 cup olive oil
1 sweet yellow (Spanish) onion,
    thinly sliced
2 garlic cloves, pressed
1 small bunch fresh parsley, chopped
6 sun-dried tomatoes, chopped
1 oregano or thyme sprig, optional
1 bay leaf
2 stalks celery, coarsely chopped
3 carrots, coarsely chopped
1 red bell pepper, coarsely chopped
1 (12-oz.) can chickpeas
    (garbanzo beans)
1 (12-oz.) can cannellini beans (a white
    kidney bean) or red kidney beans
1 (28-oz.) can Italian plum tomatoes,
    crushed
8 cups water
8 oz. cheese tortellini
Salt and pepper to taste
1/4 lb. locatelli or Parmesan cheese,
    freshly grated

In a large soup pot, heat olive oil. Add onion, garlic, parsley, sun-dried tomatoes, oregano or thyme and bay leaf. Sauté 10 minutes, stirring often. Add celery, carrots and pepper and sauté another 5 minutes. Add chickpeas (garbanzo beans), beans, crushed tomatoes and water. Cover and bring to a boil. Reduce heat and simmer, covered 1-1/2 hours. Add tortellini and simmer uncovered 25 minutes. Remove bay leaf. Ladle soup into individual bowls, season with salt and pepper to taste. Top with a generous serving of cheese.

*A*n exquisite blending of flavors. Delicious served with
a loaf of crusty bread.

Serves 6 to 8

**3 tablespoons oil from sun-dried
   tomatoes**
**1/2 large sweet yellow (Spanish) onion,
   coarsely chopped**
7 sun-dried tomatoes
2 fennel bulbs, coarsely chopped
2 cups chicken broth
4 cups water
1/2 cup freshly grated Parmesan cheese
1/2 cup half and half
Salt and pepper to taste

Heat olive oil in a large pot. Add onion and sun-dried tomatoes and sauté 5 minutes. Add fennel and sauté another 5 minutes. Add broth and water. Cover, bring to a boil, then reduce heat and simmer 20 minutes. Remove pot from heat and with a slotted spoon remove all vegetables and place them in a food processor or blender. Reserve broth. Purée vegetables and return them to the pot. Add grated cheese and half and half. Stir well and season to taste with salt and pepper. Serve immediately.

A rich and robust soup . . . the sun-dried tomatoes add a subtle flavor.

Serves 6 to 8

**1 lb. dry navy beans or 2 (1-lb.) cans
    white beans with liquid**
6 cups water
1/4 cup olive oil
4 garlic cloves, pressed
**1 small sweet yellow (Spanish) onion,
    peeled, thinly sliced**
6 sun-dried tomatoes, chopped
2 stalks celery, chopped
1 small bunch fresh parsley, chopped
**1 small rosemary, thyme or marjoram
    sprig or dried herbs, optional**
Salt and pepper to taste
4 cups chicken broth
1 medium head escarole, chopped
**1/4 lb. locatelli or Parmesan cheese,
    freshly grated**

If using dry beans, place them in a large soup pot. Cover with water and soak overnight. Drain and discard water. Add 6 cups fresh water and bring to a boil. Reduce heat and simmer covered 1 hour. If using canned beans, put them in pot. Pour olive oil in a skillet and heat. Add garlic, onion and sun-dried tomatoes and sauté 5 minutes. Add celery, parsley and herbs and sauté another 5 minutes. Add this to the beans, with salt, pepper and chicken broth. Cover and simmer 1-1/2 hours, stirring occasionally. Add chopped escarole. Simmer 30 minutes, adjust seasonings and serve with grated cheese.

Vegetables

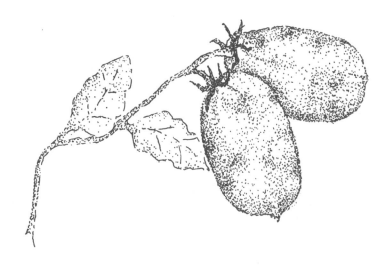

Fennel or Finocchio is an exceptionally flavorful vegetable too frequently overlooked. It can be eaten raw in a salad or sautéed as in this savory dish.

Serves 4

3 large fennel bulbs
1/4 cup olive oil
2 sun-dried tomatoes, chopped
1/4 cup white wine
1/4 cup water
Salt to taste
4 tablespoons freshly grated
**   Parmesan cheese**

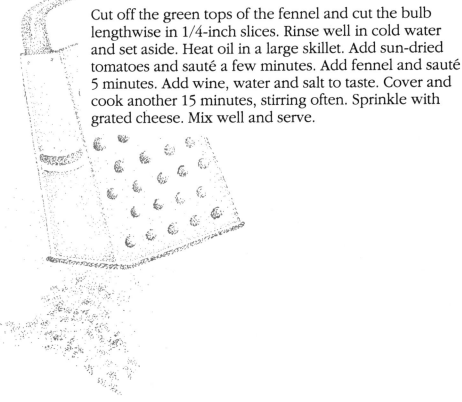

Cut off the green tops of the fennel and cut the bulb lengthwise in 1/4-inch slices. Rinse well in cold water and set aside. Heat oil in a large skillet. Add sun-dried tomatoes and sauté a few minutes. Add fennel and sauté 5 minutes. Add wine, water and salt to taste. Cover and cook another 15 minutes, stirring often. Sprinkle with grated cheese. Mix well and serve.

The creamy texture and mellow flavor of mozzarella and the sweetness of the sun-dried tomatoes are well suited in this simple but tempting strudel.

Serves 4 to 6

8 sun-dried tomatoes, chopped
1/2 cup coarsely chopped fresh basil
4 cups grated mozzarella
2 cups freshly grated
  Parmesan cheese
Salt and pepper to taste
10 phyllo sheets, defrosted
1/2 cup butter

Make filling by combining sun-dried tomatoes, basil, mozzarella, Parmesan cheese, salt and pepper together in a bowl. Set aside. Unroll the package of phyllo and peel off 10 sheets. Set them aside on a piece of plastic wrap and cover with a layer of plastic wrap to prevent phyllo from drying out. Reroll the remaining sheets and either refrigerate or freeze. Melt butter in small saucepan. Take 1 sheet of phyllo and lay flat on dish towel. Using a small pastry brush, brush entire phyllo sheet lightly with butter. Repeat until you have 5 sheets, stacked one on top of another. Preheat oven to 375F (190C). Spread half the filling lengthwise along the longer edges of the phyllo; roll up as a jelly roll. Place seam side down on an oiled baking sheet; lightly score top in several places. Repeat this process with remaining phyllo. Place in oven and bake 20 to 25 minutes until crisp and golden brown. Cut in serving-size pieces and serve hot. To serve as an appetizer, cut into small pieces.

*S*avory with the rustic flavor of wild
mushrooms . . . this tart makes a lovely presentation.

Serves 4

Pastry:
1-1/2 cups flour
1/2 teaspoon salt
1/2 cup unsalted butter, cut into
　　small pieces
3 tablespoons ice water

Filling:
1/4 cup Balsamic vinegar
1/4 cup water
1/2 oz. dried porcini mushrooms
3 tablespoons virgin olive oil
2 garlic cloves, minced
1 small onion, minced
1/2 lb. fresh shiitake mushrooms,
　　rinsed and sliced
1/2 lb. crimini mushrooms, rinsed
　　and sliced
Salt and pepper to taste
4 sun-dried tomatoes, chopped
1/4 cup finely chopped fresh
　　flat-leaf parsley
3 eggs, beaten
3/4 cup heavy cream
1/2 cup freshly grated mozzarella
1/2 cup freshly grated Parmesan cheese

Make pastry with a food processor or by hand. Process flour, salt and butter and while machine is running add water. Process until the mixture holds together. Wrap in plastic wrap and chill 1 hour. Preheat oven to 375F (190C). Roll out dough on lightly floured surface. Place dough in a 9-inch tart pan with removable bottom. Freeze 5 to 10 minutes. Line the pastry shell with aluminum foil and some dried beans to weigh it down. Bake 20 minutes. Remove foil and beans; set crust aside to cool.

Heat vinegar and water in a small saucepan, add porcini mushrooms. Set aside 20 minutes. Heat olive oil in skillet, add garlic, onions, shiitake and crimini mushrooms and sauté 5 minutes. Add porcini mushrooms with liquid, salt and pepper to taste and simmer uncovered 15 minutes. Remove from heat and stir in sun-dried tomatoes and parsley. Beat together eggs and cream; blend in cheeses. Add mushroom mixture and pour in tart shell. Bake 1/2 hour. Cool slightly before cutting and serving.

*E*ggplant, once known as mala insana or "mad apple," seems to be enjoying a resurgence in popularity and appeal these days. We especially like the Japanese variety that has fewer seeds, but the classic firm ripe eggplant performs well in all respects. The following can be served as a main dish or as an accompaniment.

Serves 4

1 medium eggplant, peeled, cubed
1/2 cup water
6 sun-dried tomatoes, finely chopped
1 small onion, finely chopped
1 large garlic clove, pressed
2 tablespoons chopped fresh parsley
2 tablespoons chopped fresh basil
Salt and pepper to taste
1 egg, lightly beaten
3 tablespoons freshly grated
  Parmesan cheese
1/2 to 1 cup unseasoned bread crumbs
Oil for frying

Simmer eggplant in salted water until tender, about
5 minutes. Drain well in colander, pressing out all
excess water with a spoon. Transfer into a blender
or food processor and blend until smooth. Place in a
medium bowl and add remaining ingredients except
oil. Mix well. Heat oil in a heavy skillet. Form eggplant
mixture in patties and fry on both sides until golden
brown, about 5 minutes on each side. Drain on a paper
towel and serve at once.

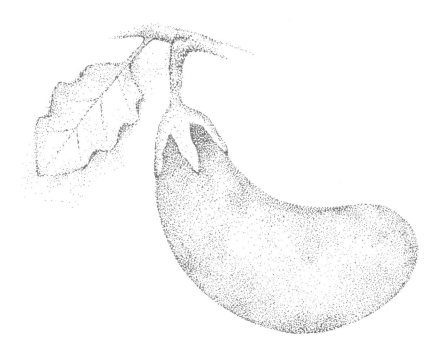

*T*his Greek classic is transformed by the addition of a
few special ingredients.

Serves 6

**3 (10-oz.) packages frozen
  chopped spinach**
1/2 cup lightly salted butter
**1/2 large sweet yellow (Spanish) onion,
  sliced**
4 large garlic cloves, pressed
4 sun-dried tomatoes, chopped
1 small parsley sprig, chopped
1/2 lb. mushrooms, sliced
1/2 cup pine nuts
1/2 lb. feta cheese, crumbled
Juice of 1 lemon
Salt and pepper to taste
**1 (1-lb.) package phyllo dough,
  defrosted**
Olive oil

Preheat oven to 350F (175C). Cook spinach as directed. Drain in colander, pressing with a spoon to extract all liquid. Set aside. In a large skillet, melt butter on low heat. Add onion, garlic and sun-dried tomatoes. Sauté about 7 minutes. Add parsley, mushrooms and pine nuts. Mix well and sauté another 5 minutes. Add feta cheese, lemon juice and spinach to the skillet. Season to taste with salt and pepper and mix. Unwrap 21 sheets of phyllo. Generously oil a 14" x 9" baking dish with olive oil. Place 7 sheets of phyllo in the prepared dish. Spoon 1/2 the spinach mixture evenly over the phyllo. Repeat with 7 more phyllo sheets and the remaining spinach. Place the last 7 sheets on top and brush generously with olive oil. Bake 35 to 40 minutes. Remove from oven and cool 10 minutes before cutting.

Greens of all kinds delight us. A platter piled high with glossy greens is a beautiful sight. This tasty dish can be served hot or at room temperature, as a light lunch or as an accompaniment to a larger meal. Serve with a crusty baguette to dip in the flavorful juice.

Serves 4

1 large or 2 small heads escarole, washed, chopped
1 cup water
3 tablespoons olive oil
5 whole garlic cloves, peeled
2 canned flat anchovy fillets, finely chopped, optional
5 sun-dried tomatoes, coarsely chopped
Salt and pepper to taste

Put chopped escarole in a medium-size pot and add 1 cup water. Cover and steam 10 minutes. Drain in colander, pressing out any excess water with a spoon. Heat olive oil in a large skillet and add garlic and anchovy. Sauté until garlic turns golden and anchovies dissolve. Add escarole, sun-dried tomatoes, salt and pepper; cover. Simmer on medium heat 10 minutes. Remove garlic cloves with a spoon and discard. Serve.

*W*e *prepare this delightful dish at the end of every summer when peppers are abundant. We like to use several varieties of peppers ranging from mild to hot. However if you can only find red bell peppers and a little hot pepper, that will do quite nicely. We usually make large batches as we find they freeze well. You can remove individual portions from the freezer during the year to add to sandwiches, pasta, omelettes and a number of other different meals.*

Makes about 2 to 3 portions

2 red bell peppers
1 orange bell pepper
1 yellow bell pepper
1 hot chili pepper
4 tablespoons olive oil
3 large garlic cloves, pressed
7 sun-dried tomatoes, chopped
1 scant teaspoon salt

Wash, core and slice all peppers into strips. Heat olive oil in a skillet and add garlic and peppers. Sauté on low heat 20 minutes, stirring often. Add sun-dried tomatoes and salt. Sauté another 10 minutes and serve.

If you have fresh plum tomatoes in your garden, use them instead of canned.

Serves 6 to 8

Vegetable Medley:
3 tablespoons extra-virgin olive oil
4 large garlic cloves, minced
1 sweet yellow (Spanish) onion, sliced
5 sun-dried tomatoes, chopped
1 small bunch flat-leaf parsley, chopped
3 fresh basil leaves, chopped
1 red bell pepper, sliced
1 Hungarian hot wax pepper, sliced
1 medium eggplant, peeled, cubed
1 zucchini, cubed
2 tablespoons olivada, optional
1 (28-oz.) can whole plum tomatoes
1/4 cup dry sherry or white wine
Salt and pepper to taste

Polenta:
6 cups water
1 teaspoon salt
2 cups coarse cornmeal
1/4 cup butter
1/2 cup freshly grated Parmesan cheese

Heat olive oil in a large skillet. Add garlic, onion, sun-dried tomatoes, parsley and basil. Sauté 10 minutes. Add peppers, eggplant and zucchini; stir and sauté 5 minutes. Add olivada if desired, tomatoes and wine. Stir and simmer uncovered 40 minutes. Season to taste with salt and pepper.

Bring water and salt to a boil. Reduce to a simmer and add cornmeal in a slow stream, stirring with a spoon as you pour. Cook on low simmer 15 to 20 minutes, stirring constantly. When polenta is finished, remove from heat and add butter and grated cheese. Mix well and spoon into individual serving bowls, topping with a generous serving of vegetables and sauce. Serve immediately.

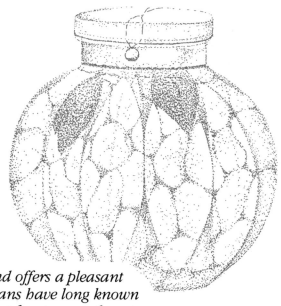

ᴥ *Polenta is a staple of Italy and offers a pleasant change from pasta. The Italians have long known that it is a perfect complement for strong, vibrant flavors such as Italian cheeses, spices and peppers.*

*T*his is a variation of eggplant Parmesan. The eggplant is coated with an egg batter rather than breaded. The addition of sun-dried tomatoes in the sauce lends a subtle sweet flavor.

Serves 4

Sauce:
2 (28-oz.) cans crushed tomatoes
4 sun-dried tomatoes
3 garlic cloves, minced
4 tablespoons virgin olive oil
1/4 cup finely chopped flat-leaf parsley
3 tablespoons chopped fresh basil
leaves or 1 teaspoon dried basil leaves

2 Japanese eggplants or 1 medium
eggplant, cut into 1/2-inch slices
Salt
1 cup unbleached or all-purpose flour
1 teaspoon dried parsley
1 teaspoon salt
3 eggs beaten
1/4 cup half and half
About 1/2 cup olive oil for frying
1 cup freshly grated Parmesan cheese
1/2 lb. mozzarella, freshly grated

To prepare sauce, purée both types of tomatoes in blender or processor. Sauté garlic in oil until golden. Add tomato purée, parsley and basil. Simmer, uncovered, until sauce thickens, about 45 minutes. Set aside.

Place eggplant slices on paper towels and salt. Let sit 10 minutes. Mix flour in a large dish with parsley and 1 teaspoon salt. Beat eggs and half and half in a small bowl. Dry eggplant slices with paper towels. Individually dredge in flour mixture and dip in egg mixture. Heat olive oil in skillet. Fry each slice until golden brown, remove and drain on paper towels. Arrange eggplant slices in an oiled 1-1/2 qt. soufflé dish. Sprinkle first layer with Parmesan and mozzarella. Continue layering until all eggplant slices are used, ending with Parmesan on top. Bake in 350F (175C) oven until top is browned, about 40 minutes. Remove from oven and cool 10 minutes. To unmold timbale, loosen edges with knife blade. Shake gently and invert onto a serving platter. Cut in wedges; spoon sauce over individual servings.

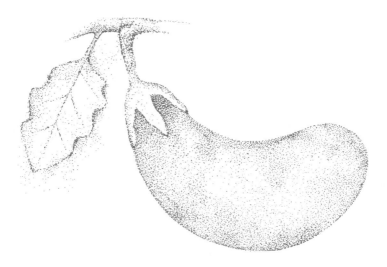

Look for Italian sweet red peppers for this dish. In creating the recipe we used a long sweet Italia Corno di Toro "horn of the bull" which was growing in splendid abundance in the garden.

Serves 6

6 large Italian sweet red peppers or
  red bell peppers
1/4 cup extra-virgin olive oil
2 garlic cloves, pressed
6 sun-dried tomatoes, finely chopped
1 tablespoon finely chopped parsley
1/4 cup freshly grated Parmesan cheese
1/4 cup freshly grated Fontina cheese
1/2 cup unseasoned bread crumbs
2 small or 1 medium zucchini,
  finely chopped
Salt and pepper to taste
4 tablespoons white wine

Preheat oven to 400F (205C). Cut peppers in half lengthwise. Remove seeds and core. Oil a large oven-proof baking dish. Combine olive oil, garlic, sun-dried tomatoes, parsley, cheeses, bread crumbs, zucchini, salt and pepper in a large bowl. Mix well. Stuff pepper halves with the mixture, mounding generously. Pour wine in the bottom of the baking dish. Place peppers in baking dish and place in oven. Bake until peppers are tender and stuffing has formed a golden crust, about 40 minutes. Serve immediately.

This recipe was given to us by our friend Mary Vavrek, who has a large following in this area due to her excellent cooking talents and her warm heart.

Serves 4 to 6

1 lb. fresh green beans, tips removed
2 tablespoons butter
2 tablespoons olive oil
4 garlic cloves, pressed
8 sun-dried tomatoes, finely chopped
2 tablespoons bread crumbs
2 tablespoons freshly grated locatelli or
   Parmesan cheese
Salt and pepper to taste

Rinse beans and place in a pot. Cover and blanch 3 to 4 minutes. Drain and set aside. Heat butter and olive oil in a skillet. Add garlic and sun-dried tomatoes and sauté 3 minutes. Add beans, bread crumbs and cheese. Mix and remove from heat. Add salt and pepper to taste and serve.

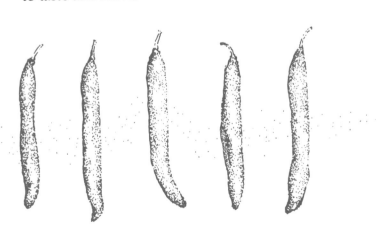

The fresh vegetables and herbs for this colorful ratatouille were gathered from a bountiful late summer's garden. A tossed green salad and loaf of sourdough bread completes this delectable meal.

Serves 4

1/2 cup olive oil
5 garlic cloves, pressed
1 large onion, peeled and chopped
2 Japanese eggplants or 1 medium
**   eggplant, peeled, cubed**
3 small zucchini, sliced
6 ripe plum tomatoes,
**   coarsely chopped**
7 sun-dried tomatoes,
**   coarsely chopped**
2 Italian sweet red peppers, seeded,
**   sliced into strips**
Chopped fresh basil, flat-leaf parsley
**   and marjoram, to taste**
Salt and pepper to taste
1/2 cup freshly grated
**   Parmesan cheese**

Heat olive oil in a large skillet. Add garlic and onions, sauté 5 minutes. Add eggplant and sauté 5 to 7 minutes more. Add remaining ingredients except cheese. Cover and simmer 15 to 20 minutes or until vegetables are tender. Add cheese, mix well and serve.

A unique blend of ingredients. Try serving it on a generous portion of lettuce as a warm salad, an appetizer or to accompany meat or fowl.

Serves 4

3 tablespoons olive oil
1 garlic clove, minced
1/2 medium onion, sliced
4 sun-dried tomatoes, finely chopped
3-1/2 oz. shiitake mushrooms
2 heads radicchio, cut into thin shreds
2 tablespoons Balsamic vinegar
Salt and pepper to taste

Heat olive oil in a medium skillet. Add garlic, onion and sun-dried tomatoes, sauté 5 minutes. Add shiitake mushrooms, radicchio and vinegar and sauté 10 minutes. Season to taste with salt and pepper and serve.

A frittata is an Italian open-faced omelette that is simple to make, has many variations and makes an impressive breakfast, brunch, lunch or light dinner.

Serves 4

2 tablespoons olive oil
1/2 sweet yellow (Spanish) onion,
   thinly sliced
1/2 lb. fresh mushrooms, washed,
   sliced
6 sun-dried tomatoes, chopped
1 bunch fresh flat-leaf parsley,
   chopped
1 oregano or thyme sprig or
   1/2 teaspoon dried oregano or
   thyme leaves
2 tablespoons dry white or red wine
Salt and pepper to taste
6 extra large eggs
1/4 lb. mozzarella, cut into
   small pieces

Heat olive oil in a heavy oven-proof skillet (preferably cast iron). Add onion and sauté 5 minutes, then add mushrooms, sun-dried tomatoes, parsley, oregano or thyme, wine, salt and pepper. Sauté about 8 minutes. Beat eggs in a bowl and pour over vegetables and reduce heat to very low. Place mozzarella pieces evenly over eggs and cook uncovered about 10 minutes. Remove skillet from stove top and place under broiler 5 minutes. Cut in 4 wedges and serve.

*V*egetables can be grilled several different ways.
*You can place them directly on the grill, or you can
wrap them in foil and place the foil packet on the grill.
They are both good yet very different. Here is a recipe
for vegetables grilled in foil.*

Serves 4 to 6

**1 medium eggplant, peeled, cut into
   bite-size pieces**
1/2 lb. mushrooms, washed, cut in half
**1 medium zucchini, cut into
   bite-size pieces**
1 red bell pepper, cut into rings
1 red onion, cut into rings
3 sun-dried tomatoes, chopped
1 garlic clove, pressed
1/4 cup olive oil
1 teaspoon salt

Place vegetables in a large bowl. Add sun-dried tomatoes, garlic, olive oil and salt. Mix well and refrigerate 2 to 3 hours. Spoon vegetables and any liquid that is on the bottom of the bowl into a large piece of aluminum foil. Close by pinching foil edges together over vegetables. Place on a hot grill 45 minutes. Open foil, the vegetables should be tender and juicy. Pour in a bowl and serve. If you are not grilling, bake in a hot 350F (175C) oven 45 minutes.

Pasta, Risottos,
Bread & Pizzas

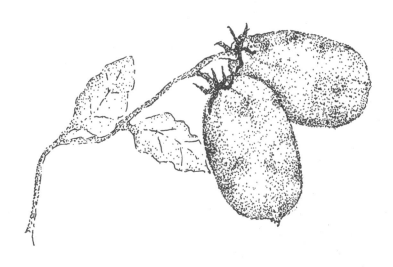

Makes a lovely holiday dinner. We make our own
crepes, but if you wish you can bypass that step and
use a good-quality manicotti shell.

Makes 10 large crepes generously serving
5 or more people

Sauce:
4 tablespoons olive oil
6 large garlic cloves, pressed
1 (2-lb.) can crushed Italian plum
   tomatoes
1/2 cup dry white wine
3-5 fresh basil leaves, finely chopped
3 sprigs fresh parsley
1/2 teaspoon salt

Filling:
1 (10-oz.) package frozen chopped
  spinach
2 lb. ricotta cheese
12 sun-dried tomatoes, chopped
1/2 cup freshly grated locatelli or
  Parmesan cheese
Black pepper to taste

Crepes:
6 large eggs, beaten
2 cups flour
1/2 cup water
1/2 teaspoon salt

1/4 lb. locatelli or Parmesan cheese,
  freshly grated

Heat olive oil in a skillet and add garlic. Sauté 5 minutes. Add tomatoes, wine, herbs and salt. Simmer uncovered while you prepare the filling and crepes.

Cook spinach as directed on package and drain well. Place in a large bowl together with ricotta, sun-dried tomatoes and grated locatelli or Parmesan cheese. Add pepper to taste, mix well and set aside.

Preheat oven to 350F (175C). To make crepes: Place eggs in a large bowl and beat well. Add flour and beat again until well-incorporated. Add water and salt. Beat again and set aside. The batter should be the consistency of heavy cream. Brush an 8-inch skillet lightly with olive oil and then pour in about 4 table-spoons batter. Rotate skillet quickly so that batter spreads out evenly over the entire surface of pan. Cook on low heat until the top is dry, remove from pan. Pour in another 4 tablespoons and repeat the process until all the batter is used. As each crepe is finished, fill with about 5 tablespoons filling and roll up and place in a lightly oiled baking pan. When all crepes have been filled, spoon sauce over top and sprinkle with locatelli or Parmesan cheese. Bake 40 minutes and serve immediately.

*H*ere is another wonderful yet simple way to serve
pasta. From start to finish it takes about the same amount
of time as it does to cook the pasta.

Serves 4

1 lb. fusilli
3 tablespoons olive oil
4 large garlic cloves, pressed
1 teaspoon anchovy paste
1 tablespoon capers
7 sun-dried tomatoes, chopped
3 leaves fresh basil, chopped or
  1 teaspoon dried basil leaves
1 small bunch flat-leaf parsley, chopped
1 red bell pepper, sliced
3 Hungarian hot waxed, Karlo or red
  cherry peppers, sliced
4 ripe tomatoes, chopped
1 cup dry white wine or sherry
1 tablespoon olivada or 1 tablespoon
  chopped Kalamata or Niçoise olives
1/2 cup water
Salt to taste
2 tablespoons butter
1/4 lb. Parmesan cheese, freshly grated

Begin cooking fusilli as directed. Heat olive oil in a large skillet, add garlic, anchovy paste, capers, sun-dried tomatoes, basil and parsley. Sauté 5 minutes. Add peppers, tomatoes, wine, olivada or olives, water and salt. Cover and simmer 15 minutes. Remove from heat and stir in butter. Drain pasta and return to pot. Add sauce and cheese and toss to combine. Serve immediately.

A *classic combination of flavors.*

Serves 3 to 4

1/2 oz. dried porcini mushrooms
2 cups heavy cream
1/2 lb. asparagus spears, trimmed,
**   rinsed and cut into 1/2-inch pieces**
2 tablespoons virgin olive oil
1 tablespoon butter
1 garlic clove, minced
6 sun-dried tomatoes, coarsely chopped
1/4 lb. thinly sliced prosciutto, cut into
**   small strips**
Salt and freshly ground pepper to taste
1 lb. fresh linguine
1/4 cup chopped fresh flat-leaf parsley
1 cup freshly grated Parmesan cheese

Cover porcini mushrooms in warm water and soak
1 hour. Drain and cut into thin slivers. In a medium
saucepan simmer cream over low heat 10 minutes or
until reduced by about half. Place asparagus in a skillet,
add water and steam 8 minutes. Do not overcook. Set
aside. Pour oil in a medium-size skillet, add butter and
sauté garlic, porcini, sun-dried tomatoes and prosciutto
several minutes. Add salt and pepper to taste. Now add
asparagus and cream, stir and simmer over low heat
5 minutes. Cook linguine as directed. Drain and add
cream sauce immediately. Add parsley and Parmesan
cheese and toss to combine. Serve immediately.

A truly magnificent sauce!

Serves 2 to 4

4 teaspoons olive oil
5 large garlic cloves, pressed
1 small sweet yellow (Spanish) onion, sliced
1 small bunch fresh parsley, chopped
5 sun-dried tomatoes, chopped
1 or 2 red hot peppers, crumbled
1 lb. Portobello mushrooms, chopped
1 (2-lb.) can whole Italian plum tomatoes
Pinch of sugar
Salt to taste

1 to 1-1/2 lb. rigatoni or other pasta
1/4 lb. locatelli or Parmesan cheese, freshly grated

Heat olive oil in a large skillet. Add garlic, onion, parsley, sun-dried tomatoes and hot peppers. Sauté 10 minutes. Add Portobello mushrooms and sauté 5 minutes. Add tomatoes, crushing them as you pour them into the pan. Add a little sugar and salt to taste. Simmer uncovered 1 hour on low heat, stirring occasionally. Cook pasta as directed and drain. Spoon sauce over pasta and serve. Pass a bowl of locatelli or Parmesan cheese.

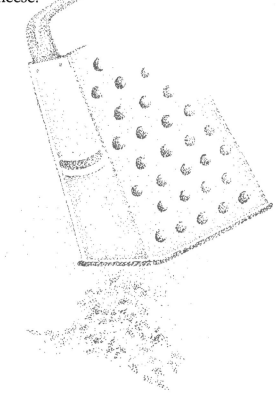

A simple, yet delectable creation requiring little time to prepare.

Serves 3 to 4

1/2 cup extra-virgin olive oil
4 large garlic cloves, pressed
12 shiitake mushrooms, sliced
5 sun-dried tomatoes, chopped
1 tablespoon oil from sun-dried
  tomato jar
6 artichoke hearts packed in water,
  drained, sliced
12 pitted large black olives
1 teaspoon anchovy paste, optional
1 small bunch fresh parsley, chopped
1 lb. linguine
1/4 lb. locatelli or Parmesan cheese,
  freshly grated
Salt and pepper to taste

Pour olive oil in a large skillet and heat. Add garlic, shiitake mushrooms and sun-dried tomatoes. Pour about 1 tablespoon oil from the sun-dried tomatoes into the pan. Sauté 5 minutes, then add artichoke hearts, olives, anchovy paste and parsley. Stir well, making sure anchovy paste is well incorporated. Sauté on low heat, uncovered another 5 minutes. Cook linguine as directed and drain. Place in a large serving bowl. Add grated cheese and toss well. Then add the ingredients from the skillet and toss again. Season to taste with salt and pepper and serve immediately.

A luscious contrast of tastes and textures.

Serves 2 to 4

1/4 cup extra-virgin olive oil
4 large garlic cloves, crushed
**1/2 lb. crimini mushrooms, washed,
  sliced**
6 sun-dried tomatoes, chopped
1 red bell pepper, sliced
1 small bunch fresh parsley, chopped
1/4 cup pine nuts
6 pitted large black olives, sliced
1 lb. cheese or meat tortellini
**1/4 lb. locatelli or Parmesan cheese,
  freshly grated**

Pour olive oil in a large skillet and heat slowly. Add garlic, mushrooms, sun-dried tomatoes, red pepper, parsley, pine nuts and olives. Sauté 15 minutes. Cook tortellini as directed. Drain tortellini and place in a bowl. Add mushroom mixture and toss well. Serve immediately. Pass a bowl of grated locatelli or Parmesan.

This is our own version of pesto using sun-dried tomatoes instead of basil. You can enjoy sesto year round whereas pesto is limited to when fresh basil is available. Try it, it's really spectacular!

Serves 3 to 4

1/4 cup lightly salted butter
8 sun-dried tomatoes
1/4 lb. sharp Italian cheese,
    cut in quarters
4 tablespoons olive oil
1/2 cup pine nuts
1 small bunch parsley
2 fresh basil leaves

1 to 1-1/2 lb. pasta

Melt butter in a small pan on low heat. Place remaining ingredients in a food processor or blender. Process and add melted butter as it whirls into a thick sauce. Set aside. Cook pasta as directed. Drain pasta and return to cooking pot. Add sesto and mix well. Serve immediately.

We hope the purists will forgive us, but we were able to turn this once-very-rich repast to one that is kinder to our hearts. The addition of sun-dried tomatoes offered so much flavor that we cut back the amount of salted meat. We prefer the leaner prosciutto to the traditional pancetta (Italian bacon). Also, we make this dish with fewer eggs than traditionally used.

Serves 3 to 4

1 lb. spaghetti
2 tablespoons oil from sun-dried
   tomato jar
1/4 lb. prosciutto, chopped
6 sun-dried tomatoes, chopped
1/2 cup light cream
2 eggs
1 cup freshly grated Parmesan cheese
Black pepper to taste

Cook spaghetti as directed. Heat oil in a skillet and add
prosciutto and sun-dried tomatoes. Sauté 5 minutes.
Beat cream and eggs together in a bowl and set aside.
Drain pasta and return to pot. Add prosciutto and
sun-dried tomatoes, mix. Then add cream and eggs, stir
quickly to mix well. Add cheese and black pepper, toss
well and serve immediately.

This is a simple and perfect pasta to prepare when the summer temperature's rising and the garden yields a profusion of red ripe tomatoes and fresh basil.

Serves 3 to 4

5 tablespoons virgin olive oil
2 garlic cloves, minced
1 small onion, minced
5 large ripe tomatoes, coarsely
    chopped, reserve liquid
3 sun-dried tomatoes, finely chopped
1/2 cup coarsely chopped fresh basil
4 tablespoons red wine vinegar
Salt and freshly ground pepper to taste
1 lb. cappeletti
1 tablespoon virgin olive oil
Freshly grated Parmesan cheese

Heat 1 tablespoon olive oil in small skillet over medium heat. Add garlic and onion and sauté 3 minutes; do not brown. Transfer to large bowl. Mix in tomatoes with liquid, remaining 4 tablespoons olive oil, sun-dried tomatoes, basil and vinegar. Season with salt and pepper. Cover and let stand 3 to 6 hours at room temperature. Just before serving, cook cappeletti as directed; drain and transfer to large serving bowl. Add 1 tablespoon olive oil and toss well. Add sauce and toss well again. Sprinkle with cheese and serve.

*A*n *exhilarating tomato sauce that is quick and easy to prepare.*

Serves 2 to 4

1/4 cup extra-virgin olive oil
2 small dried hot red peppers,
   crumbled
6 sun-dried tomatoes, chopped
4 large garlic cloves, pressed
1/2 teaspoon anchovy paste, optional
1 small bunch fresh parsley, chopped
2 or 3 fresh basil leaves or
   1/2 teaspoon dried basil leaves
1 tablespoon sugar
Salt to taste
1 (2-lb.) can whole plum tomatoes
1 lb. ziti or other pasta
1/4 lb. locatelli or Parmesan cheese,
   freshly grated

Heat olive oil in a large skillet. Add hot peppers, crushing with your fingers. Sauté 5 minutes. Add sun-dried tomatoes, garlic, anchovy paste, parsley, basil, sugar and a little salt. Sauté 5 minutes. Add canned tomatoes, crushing them as you pour them into the pan. Stir and simmer uncovered 1 hour. The sauce thickens as it cooks. Cook ziti as directed, drain and place in individual bowls. Spoon sauce over ziti, then sprinkle a generous amount of grated locatelli or Parmesan on top.

An updated, though not quite as rich version of a classic.

Serves 4 to 6

1/4 cup butter
2 large garlic cloves
1 cup half and half
6 sun-dried tomatoes
1 to 1-1/2 lb. fettucini
1/2 lb. locatelli or Parmesan cheese,
**   freshly grated**
Salt and pepper to taste

Place butter in a small saucepan and melt on low heat. While butter is melting, place garlic, half and half and sun-dried tomatoes in a food processor or blender and blend well. Add to butter in saucepan and heat slowly while fettucini is cooking. Cook fettucini as directed and drain well. Place in a large serving bowl, pour butter sauce over top and immediately add grated cheese. Toss well and season to taste with salt and pepper. Serve immediately.

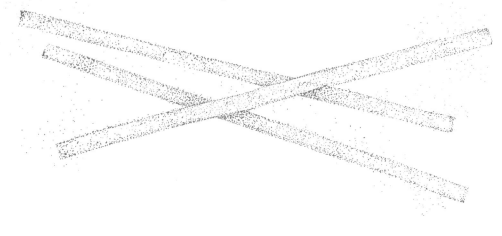

*E*legant! *Easy to prepare. Serve as a main dish with a large green salad or as a side dish with fish or fowl.*

Serves 4

4 tablespoons butter
1 large garlic clove, pressed
1 shallot, chopped
1 small onion, sliced
2 cups (1 lb.) Arborio rice
6 sun-dried tomatoes, chopped
3 cups chicken broth
2 cups water
1 cup dry white wine
1/2 cup roasted pine nuts
8 oz. Parmesan, Romano or
   Fontinella cheese, freshly grated
Salt and pepper to taste

In a heavy large pot, melt butter on low heat.
Add garlic, shallot and onion. Sauté until onion
is transparent. Add rice and mix well to coat with
butter. Add sun-dried tomatoes. Combine and heat in
a separate pot, broth, water and wine. Do not boil.
Pour in enough broth mixture to cover rice. Cook
uncovered on medium heat until most of the liquid is
absorbed, stirring often to prevent sticking. Again add
enough broth to cover, repeating this process until all
the broth has been absorbed. (This should take about
30 minutes). Add pine nuts and grated cheese. Mix well;
season with salt and pepper to taste. Serve immediately.

The fennel and sun-dried tomatoes compliment each other beautifully in this traditional rice dish of Italy.

Serves 4 to 8

2 cups chicken broth
2 cups water
1/2 cup dry sherry
1/4 cup butter
2 shallots, chopped
7 sun-dried tomatoes, chopped
1 fennel bulb, chopped
2 cups Arborio rice
1 cup freshly grated Parmesan cheese
Salt and pepper to taste

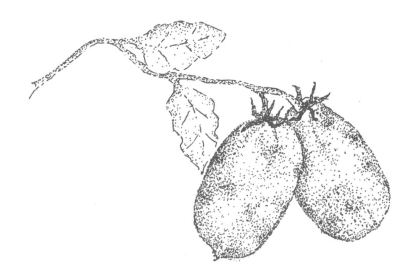

Mix chicken broth, water and sherry together in a pot and heat slowly. Melt butter in a large heavy bottom pot. Add shallots and sun-dried tomatoes and sauté 5 minutes. Add fennel and sauté another 5 minutes. Add rice and mix well. Pour in enough broth mixture to cover rice. Cook uncovered on medium heat until most of the liquid is absorbed, stirring often to prevent sticking. Again add enough broth to cover, repeating this process until all the broth has been absorbed. (This should take about 30 minutes). Add cheese and season to taste with salt and pepper. Stir well and serve immediately.

We cannot stress enough how important it is to serve risotto immediately, it becomes less palatable if allowed to sit. It doesn't do well with reheating.

*S*affron, radicchio and sun-dried tomatoes give this creamy risotto a unique appearance and flavor.

Serves 4

5 tablespoons virgin olive oil
3 shallots, finely minced
3 cups thinly sliced radicchio
6 to 7 cups chicken broth
1 teaspoon saffron threads
1 small onion, chopped
4 sun-dried tomatoes, coarsely chopped
1-1/2 cups Arborio rice
1/4 cup white wine
2 tablespoons butter
1 cup freshly grated Parmesan cheese
Salt and freshly ground pepper to taste

In a large skillet, heat 3 tablespoons olive oil. Add shallots and sauté 3 minutes. Add radicchio and continue to sauté until leaves are wilted, about 5 minutes. Transfer to plate. Heat chicken broth in a separate saucepan. Add saffron threads. Let simmer slowly. Add remaining 2 tablespoons oil to skillet and add onion and sun-dried tomatoes. Sauté several minutes. Add rice and stir 3 to 4 minutes. Stir in wine, increase heat and simmer uncovered until wine evaporates. Pour in enough broth mixture to cover rice. Cook uncovered on medium heat until most of the liquid is absorbed, stirring often to prevent sticking. Again add enough broth to cover, repeating this process until all the broth has been absorbed. (This should take about 30 minutes). Remove from heat and stir in radicchio and shallots, butter and cheese. Season to taste with salt and pepper; serve immediately.

*D*enise remembers holidays as a young girl when this delightful spinach bread was being prepared and served in her home. While making it recently she added sun-dried tomatoes to the filling and it received rave reviews.

Makes 4 loaves

Dough:
5 cups flour
1 teaspoon sugar
1 teaspoon salt
1/2 cup milk
2 cups warm water
1 (1/4-oz.) package active dry yeast
1 egg, beaten

Filling:
4 (10-oz.) packages frozen leaf spinach
4 garlic cloves, minced
3 sun-dried tomatoes, minced
1 cup pitted black olives, diced
1/4 cup virgin olive oil
Salt and freshly ground pepper to taste

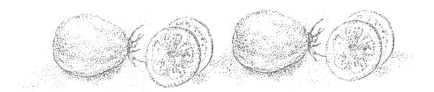

In a medium bowl combine dry ingredients. In a small saucepan bring milk to a boil then turn off immediately and pour into a separate bowl. Add 2 cups warm water and yeast and set aside. When liquid has cooled 10 minutes, add beaten egg and lightly stir. Now add flour mixture and mix well. Turn dough out onto a lightly floured board or counter top and knead several minutes. Place in large oiled bowl and cover with dampened towel and set aside in a warm spot 2 hours.

Prepare filling. Steam spinach in a small amount of water. When done drain into colander and press against spinach with a spoon to extract any extra liquid. In a medium bowl mix together spinach, garlic, sun-dried tomatoes, olives and olive oil. Add salt and pepper. Preheat oven to 350F (175C). Divide dough into 4 balls. With oiled fingers press 1 ball into a thin oval shape. Fill one side with 1/4 of spinach mixture, then close, pressing the edges together with your fingers. You now have a pocket shape. Place on an oiled baking sheet and repeat the same procedure with the remaining balls of dough. Bake about 35 to 40 minutes or until tops become golden brown. Remove from oven and enjoy!

&ebdsh; *After making one loaf you can freeze the rest of the dough to use at another time. We suggest making all four as they can be heated in the toaster for a quick lunch or frozen to enjoy at a later date.*

*B*eautiful in appearance and lusty in its appeal.

Makes 1 14" pizza or 2 small pies
Serves 4 to 6

Tomato Sauce:
2 garlic cloves, minced
1 cup diced onions
2 tablespoons olive oil
1 (28-oz.) can crushed tomatoes
1/4 cup finely chopped fresh basil
Salt and pepper to taste

Crust:
1 (1/4-oz.) package active dry yeast
1-1/3 cups warm water
3 cups durum flour or unbleached flour
3/4 cup semolina
1 teaspoon salt
1/4 cup olive oil

Toppings:
2 cups mozzarella, freshly grated
1 cup pitted black and green olives,
  sliced into rounds
10 marinated artichoke hearts,
  thinly sliced
8 sun-dried tomato slices
1 onion, cut into rings
3 tablespoons minced garlic, optional
Crushed red hot pepper flakes, optional
1-1/2 cups freshly grated
  Parmesan cheese

Slowly sauté garlic and onions in olive oil until golden, about 10 minutes. Add tomatoes, basil, salt and pepper. Simmer uncovered until thickened, about 35 minutes.

Preheat oven to 375F (190C). Combine yeast with warm water. Let sit several minutes, stir to completely dissolve. Combine flours and salt; process in food processor adding dissolved yeast and oil until dough begins to ball up. Place in a large oiled bowl. Cover and set aside in a warm spot until doubled, about 45 minutes. Punch down and remove from bowl. Divide into 2 balls for 2 round pizza pies or roll into 1 ball to make one 14" pizza. Press dough in round pizza pans with a rolling pin or by pressing by hand (our preference). Roll under 1" of the dough around the edge to make a slight rim.

Ladle tomato sauce first, spreading evenly over the crust, stopping just short of the edge. Sprinkle mozzarella evenly. Starting in the center, arrange toppings in a spiral. When cut, each slice should contain all the toppings (olives in center, artichokes next, sun-dried tomatoes, etc.). Top with Parmesan. Bake 15 minutes. If desired broil 1 minute to lightly crisp top.

‎ Variation: White Pizza

Omit tomato sauce and lightly drizzle virgin-olive oil on top of pizza dough. Add fresh minced garlic, sun-dried tomatoes, salt and pepper and toppings of your choice ending with Parmesan cheese on top. Bake 15 minutes.

A delightfully different pizza topped with spinach, feta and sun-dried tomatoes.

Serves 4 to 6

Pizza Crust, see page 98 & 99

2 tablespoons olive oil
3 large garlic cloves, pressed
1/2 large sweet yellow (Spanish) onion, chopped
1 (10-oz.) package frozen spinach
2 ripe tomatoes, sliced into thin rounds
12 pitted black olives, sliced
1/4 lb. feta cheese, crumbled
1/4 lb. mozzarella, freshly grated
7 sun-dried tomatoes, chopped
1/2 cup freshly grated Parmesan cheese

Make pizza crust as directed. When ready, roll out dough and place in baking pan. Heat olive oil in a large skillet and add garlic, onions. Sauté 5 minutes. Add spinach, cover and simmer on very low heat until spinach is defrosted. Stir well and set aside as you prepare remaining ingredients.

Preheat oven to 425F (220C). To assemble pizza, spread spinach mixture over top of crust and then evenly distribute remaining ingredients on top of spinach. Place in oven and bake 20 to 30 minutes. Check the bottom of the crust occasionally to prevent burning. It should be a golden brown when done. Slice and serve immediately.

❧ Variation: Whole-wheat Crust

Substitute 1/2 of the flour used in the pizza dough with whole-wheat flour. It makes for a heartier crust and is a welcome change.

A very good basic sauce to serve over pasta or in Braciola with Fresh Garlic, see page 138.

Makes 5 to 6 cups sauce

3 tablespoons olive oil
1 small sweet yellow (Spanish) onion,
  chopped
2 garlic cloves, minced
1/4 cup fresh basil leaves, chopped
1 (32-oz.) can tomato purée
1 (32-oz.) can crushed plum tomatoes
1 tablespoon sugar
Salt and pepper to taste

Heat olive oil in medium-size saucepan. Add onions and garlic; sauté 5 minutes. Add basil, tomato purée, crushed tomatoes and sugar. Season to taste with salt and pepper. Simmer, stirring occasionally, about 1-1/2 hours.

Seafood

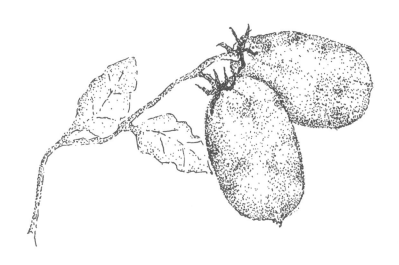

A *hearty, traditional fisherman's stew.*

Serves 4

1/2 cup olive oil
1 large onion, finely chopped
1 shallot, finely chopped
4 large garlic cloves, finely chopped
1 red cayenne pepper, finely chopped
1 Italian hot wax pepper, seeded,
    chopped
5 ripe tomatoes, coarsely chopped
4 sun-dried tomatoes, cut into
    small pieces
3 tablespoons fresh basil
2 tablespoons fresh flat-leaf parsley
1 bay leaf
1 (12-oz.) can crushed tomatoes
1-1/2 cups dry white wine
1/2 cup butter
Salt and ground pepper to taste
3 dozen littleneck clams
1 lb. large shrimp, peeled
1/2 lb. Haddock or Halibut, cut into
    1-inch pieces

Heat olive oil in large saucepan over medium heat. Add onion, shallot, garlic, cayenne pepper and hot wax pepper. Reduce heat to low. Sauté, stirring often, until vegetables are softened. Add fresh and sun-dried tomatoes, basil, parsley and bay leaf. Stir and let sauté several minutes, then add crushed tomatoes. Increase heat to medium to maintain a simmer and cook covered an hour. Uncover pan; stir in white wine, butter, salt, pepper and simmer on low heat uncovered 20 minutes. Cover and remove from heat. Place clams in sink, scrub and rinse well, to remove any sand. Rinse again and place clams in a large pot or dutch oven. Place shrimp and fish on top of clams; pour tomato sauce over seafood. Cook covered, over medium heat, shaking the pot occasionally, until clams open and fish flakes easily with a fork, about 15 minutes. Remove bay leaf. Ladle into individual soup bowls.

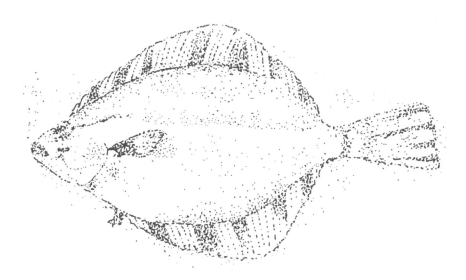

Tender scallops in a delicate tomato and basil sauce. A mixed green salad and baguette would be a nice compliment.

Serves 4

5 medium tomatoes
3 tablespoons olive oil
2 garlic cloves, minced
2 sun-dried tomatoes, finely chopped
3 tablespoons chopped fresh basil
1 teaspoon chopped fresh thyme
1 tablespoon coarsely chopped fresh
**   flat-leaf parsley**
Salt and pepper to taste
4 tablespoons butter
1-1/2 lb. bay scallops
Cooked long-grain rice

Cut tomatoes in half crosswise, then cut into 1/2-inch cubes. Heat 2 tablespoons olive oil in a skillet and add garlic, tomatoes, sun-dried tomatoes, basil, thyme, parsley, salt and pepper. Simmer about 5 minutes. Heat remaining tablespoon oil and 4 tablespoons butter in another skillet and add scallops. Sauté about 5 minutes, stirring often. Do not overcook. Add tomato sauce to the skillet with sautéed scallops and stir to mix. Serve immediately on a bed of long-grain rice.

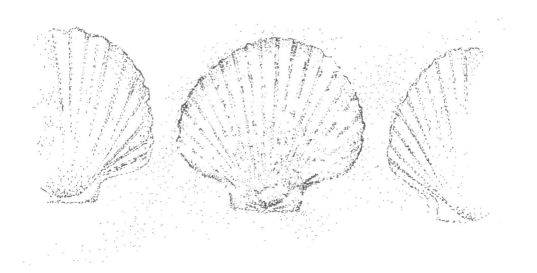

*D*ownright exciting. *Toast a slice of bread for each person and serve crabs on toast.*

Serves 2 to 3

6 soft-shell crabs, cleaned
1 cup flour
2 tablespoons butter
2 tablespoons olive oil
3 sun-dried tomatoes, chopped
2 large garlic cloves, pressed
Juice of 1/2 lemon
1/2 cup dry white wine
Salt and pepper to taste

Rinse crabs, dredge in flour and set aside. Heat butter and oil in large pan, add sun-dried tomatoes and garlic and simmer 5 minutes. Add crabs and sauté on medium heat 5 minutes on each side. Add lemon juice and wine. Season with salt and pepper. Simmer 3 minutes and serve immediately.

Halibut has a slightly sweet flavor and sun-dried tomatoes and capers serve as an interesting accent.

Serves 4

4 halibut steaks, 1-inch thick
Salt and pepper to taste
4 tablespoons butter
2 tablespoons finely chopped
**   fresh chives**
Juice of 1/2 lemon
4 tablespoons tamari soy sauce
1 teaspoon capers
2 sun-dried tomatoes, chopped

Place halibut steaks in a buttered baking dish. Sprinkle with salt and pepper and top each steak with 1 tablespoon butter. Sprinkle with chives. Combine lemon juice, tamari, capers and sun-dried tomatoes and pour over halibut steaks. Broil until fish flakes easily when tested with a fork, about 12 minutes. Serve immediately.

W*e were just about to give up on Monkfish. We
had not found a way to cook it that pleased us until
we prepared it this way.*

Serves 4

**2 lb. monkfish
2 eggs, beaten
2 tablespoons water
Juice of 1 lemon, divided
Salt and pepper to taste
1-1/2 cups flour
2 tablespoons butter
2 tablespoons olive oil
3 large garlic cloves, pressed
3 sun-dried tomatoes, chopped
1 teaspoon capers
1/2 cup dry sherry**

Cut monkfish in 1-inch pieces. In a bowl combine eggs, water, juice of 1/2 lemon and a little salt and pepper. Dip fish pieces in egg mixture then dredge with flour. Set aside. Heat butter and oil in a large pan, add garlic, sun-dried tomatoes and capers. Simmer a few minutes, then add fish. Sauté 5 minutes on each side. Add sherry and juice of 1/2 lemon and simmer 5 minutes. Season with salt and pepper and serve.

This recipe takes only minutes to prepare, and we think it is one of the finest ways to serve swordfish.

Serves 4

4 (1/2-lb.) swordfish steaks
1/4 cup olive oil
Juice of 1 lemon
Black pepper to taste
3 sun-dried tomatoes
2 large garlic cloves
4 fresh basil leaves or
   1/2 teaspoon dried basil leaves

Place swordfish in broiling pan. Pour oil evenly over fish, drizzle lemon juice on top and sprinkle with pepper. On a cutting board, chop sun-dried tomatoes, garlic and basil leaves together, forming a paste. Spread paste evenly over top of fish. Refrigerate 1 hour. Broil until fish is tender when tested (do not turn fish over!) Cooking time will vary depending on thickness of steaks: 8 to 10 minutes for 1-inch steak; 15 to 20 for 1-1/2 to 2-inch. Do not overcook. Fish should be moist and tender, not dry! Spoon pan juices over fish and serve.

A perfect summertime meal . . . grilling imparts a wonderful, distinctive flavor to seafood and vegetables.

Serves 4

Marinade:
1/2 cup olive oil
1/4 cup fresh lemon juice
5 tablespoons tamari soy sauce
1/4 teaspoon ground pepper
2 shallots, diced

8 sea scallops
2 sun-dried tomatoes, cut lengthwise
into 8 strips
12 large shrimp, peeled
2 Japanese eggplants or 1 medium
eggplant, cut crosswise into 12 pieces
1 red or yellow pepper, seeded,
quartered
2 semi-hot wax peppers, seeded, cut
into 8 pieces
2 small zucchini, cut crosswise into
12 pieces
8 pearl onions, peeled
Cooked rice

Combine marinade ingredients in small bowl and set aside. Wrap each scallop with a strip of sun-dried tomato and secure with a toothpick. Place shrimp and scallops in shallow bowl and place vegetables in another bowl. Pour 1/2 the marinade over fish and the remaining 1/2 over vegetables. Cover both and refrigerate 2 hours.

Soak wooden skewers before using. Thread kebabs by alternating vegetables with seafood on wooden skewers. Reserve any remaining marinade for basting. Oil the grill rack and prepare the grill. Grill 5 to 6 minutes on each side, basting occasionally. Serve immediately over rice.

FraDiavalo translates "hot as the devil." Try this when you need a little excitement in your life.

Serves 4

1 tablespoon butter
1 tablespoon olive oil
3 sun-dried tomatoes, coarsely chopped
5 large garlic cloves, pressed
1 small onion, sliced
1/4 cup chopped fresh flat-leaf parsley
1/2 teaspoon dried basil
2 small dried red hot peppers, crushed
2 (2-lb.) cans Italian plum tomatoes,
    liquid reserved
1/2 cup dry red wine
Salt to taste
1 teaspoon sugar
1 lb. large uncooked shrimp, peeled
1 dozen littleneck clams, scrubbed well
1 lb. linguine, cooked
1/2 lb. sharp Italian cheese,
    freshly grated

Heat butter and olive oil in a large heavy pot or skillet
with lid. Add sun-dried tomatoes, garlic, onion, parsley
and basil and sauté until onion is transparent. Crumble
hot peppers in the pot. Add tomatoes and reserved
liquid, crushing tomatoes gently as they are added. Stir
in wine, salt and sugar. Simmer on low heat uncovered
1 hour. Add shrimp, clams and cover. Raise heat to
medium and simmer until clams open. Do not
overcook! Spoon over individual servings of linguine
and sprinkle with a generous amount of cheese.

Ｗe have enhanced this classic dish with mushrooms and sun-dried tomatoes.

Serves 4

3 tablespoons butter, divided
3 sun-dried tomatoes, coarsely chopped
1/2 lb. mushrooms, rinsed, sliced
1/4 cup dry vermouth or sherry
Salt and pepper to taste
Juice of 1 lemon
2 lb. thinly sliced flounder fillets
2 eggs, beaten
1 cup flour
2 tablespoons olive oil

Melt 1 tablespoon butter in a large pan, add sun-dried tomatoes and mushrooms, sauté 5 minutes. Add vermouth or sherry and a little salt and pepper. Mix well, remove from pan and set aside. Drizzle lemon juice over fish fillets. Dip fillets in egg then dredge in flour. Melt 1 tablespoon butter and 1 tablespoon oil in the same large pan you used for sautéing. Place one layer of fillets in pan. Cook on medium heat 5 minutes on each side. Remove from pan. Add remaining butter and oil. Repeat until all fillets are cooked. Return all fillets to pan. Spoon mushrooms and sun-dried tomatoes over top. Cover and heat about 3 minutes and serve.

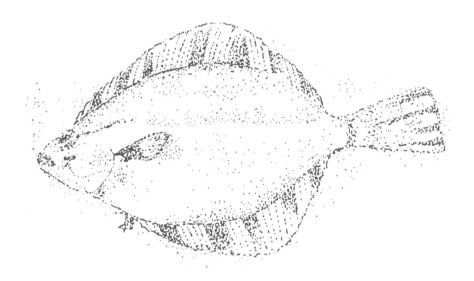

Olivada adds quite a distinctive flavor to this dish but if you can't find it, don't despair, it's great with or without it.

Serves 4

2 lb. bluefish
Juice of 1 lemon
1/2 cup dry white wine or sherry
1 teaspoon olivada
3 sun-dried tomatoes, chopped
1 medium garlic clove, pressed
1 large ripe tomato, chopped
1 small green pepper, chopped
1 tablespoon chopped fresh parsley or
  1 teaspoon dried parsley
1 sprig fresh tarragon or
  1 teaspoon dried tarragon leaves
Salt and pepper to taste
Cooked rice

Place fish on a broiling pan. In a medium bowl mix lemon juice, wine, olivada, sun-dried tomatoes and garlic. Pour mixture over fish, top with tomatoes, green pepper, parsley and tarragon. Sprinkle with salt and pepper. Place in oven. Set temperature at 350F (175C), bake 10 minutes, then place under broiler 7 minutes, or until fish tests tender. Serve at once over rice.

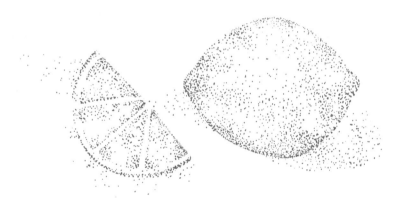

Olivada is a paste made from imported black olives. It is extremely concentrated and should be used sparingly. It can be purchased at most specialty shops.

Pasta! Crisp vegetables! Plump fresh shrimp! Primavera is quite a versatile dish.

Serves 6

1/2 cup butter, lightly salted
4 large garlic cloves, pressed
1 medium sweet yellow (Spanish)
  onion, sliced
1 head broccoli, broken in florets
1 red or green bell pepper, sliced
  into strips
2 carrots, cut into julienne strips
1/4 cup chopped fresh parsley or
  1 teaspoon dried parsley
2 sprigs fresh thyme or
  1/2 teaspoon dried thyme, optional
3-5 fresh basil leaves or
  1/2 teaspoon dried basil leaves
1-1/2 lbs. linguine
6 sun-dried tomatoes, cut into
  small pieces
1/2 cup pine nuts
1/2 cup white wine or sherry
1-1/2 lbs. large uncooked shrimp,
  peeled, rinsed
1/2 cup half and half
1/2 lb. sharp Italian cheese,
  freshly grated

In a large skillet melt butter on low heat. Add garlic and onion and sauté 5 minutes. Add vegetables, parsley and other herbs and sauté 5 more minutes. Cook linguine as directed. Add sun-dried tomatoes, pine nuts and wine to skillet mixture and simmer covered 5 more minutes or until carrots and broccoli are tender crisp. Add shrimp and half and half and sauté until shrimp are pink, about 5 minutes. Remove from heat. Drain cooked pasta and return to pot. Add vegetables and shrimp and toss well, adding grated cheese as you toss. Serve immediately.

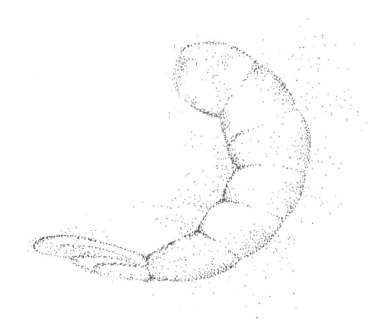

Have a loaf of crusty French bread on hand to dip in the tantalizing seasoned broth.

Serves 4

4 lb. mussels
2 cups dry white wine
4 garlic cloves, minced
1 tablespoon finely chopped
**   flat-leaf parsley**
1 tablespoon fresh tarragon or
**   1/2 tablespoon dried tarragon**
2 sun-dried tomatoes, cut into
**   small pieces**
Juice of 1 lemon
Salt and freshly ground pepper to taste
1/4 cup butter

Scrub and rinse mussels under running water. Set aside. Pour wine into a large pot. Add garlic, parsley, tarragon, sun-dried tomatoes, lemon juice, salt and pepper. Place mussels in the pot and cover tightly. Steam over medium-high heat 4 to 5 minutes. Remove open mussels with a slotted spoon. Place in individual soup bowls. Add a little bit of butter to each bowl and divide mussel broth equally. If you wish, you can strain broth through several layers of cheesecloth to catch any sand. Serve immediately.

Poultry & Meat

Simply smashing!

Serves 4

4 (1-lb.) Rock Cornish hens
Juice of 1 lemon
1/2 cup dry sherry or white wine
Salt and pepper to taste

Stuffing:
4 slices bread, cubed
1/2 cup sherry
2 tablespoons olive oil
1/2 large sweet yellow (Spanish) onion, chopped
3 large garlic cloves, pressed
1 (10-oz.) package frozen chopped spinach
1/4 cup water
6 sun-dried tomatoes, chopped
1/2 cup pistachio nuts, shelled
1/4 cup freshly grated Parmesan cheese

Preheat oven to 350F (175C). Rinse hens under cold water then put in a large baking pan. Drizzle lemon juice and wine on top and season with salt and pepper. Set aside.

Place bread cubes in a large bowl and pour sherry over top. Mix well and set aside. Heat olive oil in a large skillet and add onion and garlic. Sauté 5 minutes. Add frozen spinach and water. Cover and simmer 10 minutes until spinach is totally defrosted. Add sun-dried tomatoes, pistachios and Parmesan cheese, mix well. Add spinach mixture to the bread and mix well. Stuff into the cavities of each hen. Bake 1 hour, basting often.

Fragrant with Marsala wine and lemon, this is an elegant way to prepare chicken.

Serves 4

2 whole boned chicken breasts
1-1/2 cups unbleached flour
1 teaspoon dried parsley
1/4 teaspoon salt
2 eggs, beaten
1/2 cup half and half
1/4 cup olive oil
1/4 cup butter
1 lb. fresh mushrooms, rinsed, sliced
3 shallots, finely chopped
6 sun-dried tomatoes
Juice of 1 lemon
1/2 cup Marsala wine
Salt and freshly ground pepper to taste
Cooked Arborio rice

Trim chicken breasts, discarding skin and fat. Cut the
2 breasts into 4 pieces. Holding each piece down with
the palm of your hand, carefully slice lengthwise into
thin cutlets. Each piece should give you 2 to 3 slices.
Mix together flour, parsley and salt in a plate. In a small
flat bowl beat eggs and half and half. Dip each chicken
slice in egg mixture then dredge in flour mixture. Pour
olive oil in skillet and on medium heat lightly sauté all
slices on both sides. When coating is golden brown,
remove and place in a shallow baking dish with a lid.
Melt butter in medium-size skillet and add mushrooms,
shallots and sun-dried tomatoes. Sauté 5 minutes, then
add lemon juice and Marsala wine. Simmer gently
5 minutes then pour on top of chicken. Add salt
and pepper to taste and bake covered in a 350F (175C)
oven 30 minutes. Serve over rice.

This recipe has been in Denise's family for several generations with good reason. The red peppers and wine vinegar impart a full-bodied flavor to the chicken, and the addition of sun-dried tomatoes is a current and welcome one. Serve on a bed of Arborio rice or couscous.

Serves 4

1/4 cup virgin olive oil
1 (3-lb.) chicken, skinned, cut up
1 onion, sliced
3 medium red bell peppers, seeded,
   cut into thin slices
3 garlic cloves, minced
3 sun-dried tomatoes, diced
1 large bay leaf, broken in half
1 tablespoon chopped fresh
   flat-leaf parsley
1 sprig fresh rosemary, chopped or
   1/2 teaspoon dried rosemary
Salt and freshly ground pepper to taste
1 cup water
1/2 cup red wine vinegar

Pour oil in large unheated skillet. Place pieces of chicken in skillet and turn pieces to coat with oil. Over medium heat, brown chicken about 10 minutes. Remove chicken from pan and set aside. With the same oil in the skillet, sauté onion, peppers, garlic, sun-dried tomatoes, bay leaf, parsley, rosemary, salt and pepper 10 minutes. Return chicken to pan and simmer several minutes before adding water. Add water, cover and simmer 25 minutes. Add vinegar, cover and simmer an additional 20 to 25 minutes. Remove bay leaves. Serve on a platter, spooning all the juices and vegetables over chicken.

Stewed chicken with a sumptuous sauce served over Arborio rice or a bed of flat egg noodles.

Serves 4 to 6

1 oz. dried porcini mushrooms
1 cup water
4 teaspoons virgin olive oil
2 large garlic cloves, crushed
1 small sweet yellow (Spanish) onion, sliced
2 shallots, chopped
6 sun-dried tomatoes, cut into bite-size pieces
1 small bunch fresh parsley, chopped
1 fresh rosemary sprig, optional
1 (3 lb.) chicken, skinned, cut up
1 cup dry white or red wine
Juice of 1 lemon
Salt and pepper to taste
2 cups Arborio rice or 1 lb. egg noodles

Put dried mushrooms in a bowl and cover with 1 cup water. Let sit while you prepare the rest of the dish. In a large skillet, heat olive oil. Add garlic, onion, shallots, sun-dried tomatoes, parsley and rosemary. Sauté 10 minutes. Add chicken to skillet and cook 10 minutes, turning often. When chicken has lost its pink color, add wine, lemon juice and mushrooms, plus liquid they were soaked in. Cover skillet and simmer on low heat 45 to 50 minutes or until chicken is tender. Stir gently every 10 minutes or so and add salt and pepper to taste. Cook rice or noodles as directed. Spoon chicken and sauce over top and serve immediately.

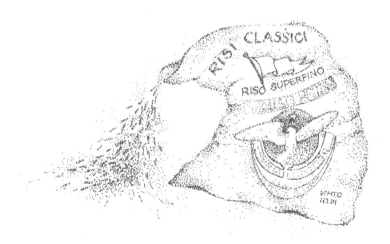

Saffron is one of our favorite spices. This is an updated version of an old favorite Denise's grandmother has been making for as long as she can remember. The distinctive flavor and vibrant saffron color is a treat to both the palate and the eye.

Serves 4

1 (3-lb.) chicken, cut up
3 tablespoons olive oil
4 whole garlic cloves
4 cups water
1 teaspoon saffron threads
1 tablespoon coarsely chopped
    fresh flat-leaf parsley
Salt and freshly ground pepper
1 cup chopped green beans
1 cup white rice
3 sun-dried tomatoes, finely diced
1-1/2 cups cooked chickpeas
    (garbanzo beans)
Salt and freshly ground pepper to taste

Rinse chicken. Leave skin on thighs and legs but trim off extra fat. Pat dry with paper towels. Heat olive oil in large pot, adding chicken and garlic cloves. Brown chicken on all sides 5 to 10 minutes. Add 4 cups water, saffron threads, parsley, salt and pepper. Cover and simmer over low heat 30 minutes. This stock will be used in the casserole. Blanch green beans; set aside. Remove chicken from stock, discarding skin and bones, and cut into bite-size pieces. Cover the bottom of a casserole with rice. Layer chicken, green beans, sun-dried tomatoes and chickpeas (garbanzo beans) on top. Pour 3 cups saffron stock over all; salt and pepper to taste and cover. Bake at 350F (175C), 40 minutes, checking once to see if more broth is needed. Add 1 cup stock if rice seems dry. Serve immediately.

Succulent roast chicken with the distinctive aroma of rosemary and bay.

Serves 4

1 (3 lb.) roasting chicken
2 teaspoons chopped fresh rosemary or
  1 teaspoon dried rosemary
1 small bay leaf
2 teaspoons chopped fresh
  flat-leaf parsley
Salt and pepper to taste
4 tablespoons olive oil
3 sun-dried tomatoes, finely chopped
1/4 cup fresh lemon juice

Preheat oven to 350F (175C). Rinse chicken thoroughly, pat dry. Rub inside and out with rosemary, bay leaf, parsley, salt and pepper. Line a baking pan with foil large enough to enclose chicken completely. Place chicken in foil, breast side up. Mix together, in small bowl, olive oil, sun-dried tomatoes and lemon juice. Pour evenly over chicken. Fold foil over chicken, crimping together to make airtight seal. Bake chicken on upper rack in oven 35 or 40 minutes. Remove chicken from oven, increase temperature to 425F (220C). Remove foil and place bird breast side down and all cooking juices back in baking pan. After 20 minutes turn bird on one side and bake 10 minutes more, then turn on other side another 10 minutes. At this point turn bird breast side up and bake a final 10 to 15 minutes. Remove bay leaf. Transfer to a serving plate and spoon all cooking juices over top. Serve immediately.

*S*un-dried tomatoes and Balsamic vinegar, a great
pairing of flavors to enhance chicken.

Serves 6

1/4 cup extra-virgin olive oil
4 large garlic cloves, pressed
1 small sweet yellow (Spanish)
   onion, sliced
6 sun-dried tomatoes, chopped
1 small bunch fresh parsley, chopped
1 fresh rosemary sprig or
   1/4 teaspoon dried rosemary
1 fresh thyme sprig or
   1/4 teaspoon dried thyme
1 small hot red pepper, crumbled
   or 1/4 teaspoon dried hot
   pepper flakes
1 (3-lb.) chicken, skinned, cut up
1/2 cup Balsamic vinegar
1/2 cup dry white or red wine
1/2 cup water
Salt to taste
2 cups Arborio rice

Pour olive oil in a large skillet and heat. Add garlic,
onion, sun-dried tomatoes, parsley, rosemary, thyme
and hot pepper. Sauté 10 minutes. Add chicken
pieces and brown slightly on both sides. Add vinegar,
wine, water and salt to taste; stir well. Cover and
simmer 45 minutes, turning chicken every 10 minutes.
While chicken is cooking, prepare rice as directed.
Spoon chicken and sauce over rice and serve.

Olivada imparts a wonderful flavor and forms a great partnership with sun-dried tomatoes.

Serves 4

1 (3-lb.) chicken, cut up

Marinade:
4 sun-dried tomatoes
1 teaspoon olivada
1 garlic clove
1/4 cup olive oil
Juice of 1 lemon
1/2 teaspoon salt
1/4 teaspoon black pepper

Rinse chicken and put in a large container with a lid. Place marinade ingredients in a food processor or blender and purée. Pour marinade over chicken, cover and refrigerate 3 hours or overnight for best flavor. When getting ready to grill, remove chicken from refrigerator and let stand at least 1/2 hour. Grill as desired, basting often with marinade.

*T*his dish is so rich in flavor that it only needs to be accompanied by a good crusty bread and a light green salad. A good dark beer would add a perfect touch.

Serves 4

1/2 oz. dried porcini mushrooms
1 cup water
4 tablespoons olive oil
3 large garlic cloves, pressed
4 (1/2-lb.) thinly cut tenderloin steaks
7 sun-dried tomatoes, chopped
1 tablespoon capers
1 small bunch flat-leaf parsley,
   chopped
1 small hot red pepper, chopped or
   1/2 teaspoon hot pepper flakes
1/2 cup dry white wine or sherry

Place porcini mushrooms in a bowl and cover with water. Soak 1/2 hour. Meanwhile, heat olive oil in a large skillet. Add garlic and sauté 5 minutes then add steaks. Sauté 5 minutes on each side, remove steaks from pan. Drain the mushrooms. Into the same pan, add sun-dried tomatoes, capers, drained mushrooms, parsley and hot pepper. Sauté 8 minutes then return steaks to the pan along with the wine. Sauté another 10 minutes, turning steaks after 5 minutes. Remove steaks from pan and place on a platter, spoon remaining sauce over top. Serve at once.

This is a wonderful version of a Southern Italian favorite. Braciola quite simply consists of a thin slice of beef, rolled with lots of fresh garlic and parsley, Parmesan cheese and sun-dried tomatoes. It is then browned in olive oil and simmered in tomato sauce.

Serves 4

Filling:
1/4 cup minced fresh garlic
2 tablespoons coarsely chopped
    fresh parsley
1/4 cup grated Parmesan cheese
4 sun-dried tomatoes, finely chopped

3/4 lb. lean top round, cut into 4 very
    thin slices
Salt and freshly ground pepper
White cotton thread
Olive oil
Marinara Sauce or see page 102

Mix together garlic, parsley, cheese and sun-dried tomatoes. Spread meat slices on counter top or cutting board. Trim and discard any excess fat. Sprinkle filling evenly over meat slices. Sprinkle with salt and pepper. Roll up meat tightly, jelly-roll fashion and, using cotton thread, tie the rolls securely. Pour olive oil in a large skillet. Over medium heat add meat rolls and brown on all sides. Remove and add to Marinara Sauce. Simmer in sauce 1 hour. Before serving remove thread by snipping with a sharp scissors and pulling out.

Enjoy this hearty fare on a cold winter's eve. Serve with a good crusty loaf of bread for dipping in the sumptuous sauce.

Serves 4 to 6

3 tablespoons olive oil
1 large sweet yellow (Spanish) onion,
  chopped
4 large garlic cloves, pressed
2 tablespoons chopped fresh
  flat-leaf parsley
4 fresh basil leaves, chopped or
  1 teaspoon dried basil leaves
1 teaspoon chopped fresh thyme or
  1 teaspoon dried thyme
1 teaspoon chopped fresh rosemary or
  1 teaspoon dried rosemary
2-1/2 lbs. beef eye roast
1 cup water
1 cup dry red wine
1/2 cup Balsamic vinegar
7 sun-dried tomatoes, coarsely chopped
8 to 10 small red new potatoes,
  quartered
4 carrots, cut into 1-inch rounds
Salt and pepper to taste

Heat olive oil in a heavy bottom pot. Add onion, garlic and herbs and sauté 5 minutes. Add beef and brown lightly on all sides. Add water and wine, cover and simmer on low heat 2 hours, turning meat every 1/2 hour. Add vinegar, sun-dried tomatoes, potatoes and carrots. Cover and continue to simmer another hour, turning meat every 15 minutes. Remove meat and cut into thin slices. Place on a serving dish together with carrots and potatoes. Spoon a little sauce over top and pass the remaining sauce. Add salt and pepper to taste.

This hearty meal is served at a crowded table at the Marina family's holiday gatherings. Serve with a crusty loaf of Italian bread, an antipasto platter and perhaps a glass of Chiaretto, an Italian Rose. This can also be served as a sauce over ziti with a little grated sharp Italian cheese.

Serves 6

**2 lbs. hot and sweet Italian sausage,
   cut into bite-size pieces**
6 tablespoons water
2 large garlic cloves, pressed
1 small onion, coarsely chopped
**2 (2-lb.) cans Italian plum tomatoes,
   coarsely chopped**
**6 sun-dried tomatoes,
   coarsely chopped**
1 small fresh parsley sprig, chopped
Salt and pepper to taste
2 tablespoons olive oil
**2 Italian sweet red peppers, cut into
   thin slices**

Place sausage pieces in a large skillet, adding about
6 tablespoons water. Fry sausage over medium heat.
The water will soon evaporate and fry sausage until
browned. Add garlic, onion, tomatoes, sun-dried
tomatoes, parsley, salt and pepper to taste. Stir and
simmer 15 to 20 minutes. Heat olive oil in a separate
skillet. Add peppers and fry quickly. Add peppers to
tomato sauce, stir and simmer another 10 to 15 minutes.
Serve immediately.

A spirited and fiery way to serve a good steak.

Serves 2 to 3

6 sun-dried tomatoes
2 garlic cloves
1 small hot red pepper or
  1/2 teaspoon hot red pepper flakes
2 (1-lb.) beef steaks

Finely chop sun-dried tomatoes, garlic and hot pepper together on a cutting board until it is a well-blended paste. Set aside. Prepare grill and place steak over hot coals. Cook on one side, turn over and spread sun-dried tomato paste evenly on the grilled side. Continue to grill until desired doneness and serve, but do not turn over again.

You *can substitute lamb or beef for the pork if you prefer. If you are unable to purchase olivada, you can chop olives such as Kalamata or Ligurian to a coarse paste.*

Serves 4 to 6

2-1/2 lbs. boneless pork loin
7 large garlic cloves, pressed
1 fresh rosemary sprig, chopped
7 black peppercorns
3 tablespoons olivada or
    3 tablespoons chopped olives
7 sun-dried tomatoes
2 tablespoons oil from sun-dried
    tomato jar
12 to 14 small red new potatoes
Salt to taste

Preheat oven to 325F (165C). Unroll pork loin and place fat side down in a baking pan. Place garlic, rosemary and peppercorns in a mortar and grind with pestle to a paste. Set aside. Spread olivada or olives evenly over pork loin and place sun-dried tomatoes evenly over olivada. Roll pork loin and tie securely with string. Cut about 7 slits in the meat and fill each slit with pepper-garlic paste. Brush meat with oil from the sun-dried tomato jar. Scrub potatoes well and place them around the meat. Sprinkle with salt to taste and bake uncovered 2 hours. Slice and serve immediately.

Glossary

Anchovies — Anchovies add a depth of flavor to foods. Depending on the dish, we use either the anchovy fillets packed in oil or anchovy paste. Use salt sparingly when using anchovies as they are quite salty.

Capers — Capers are the unopened buds of a flowering shrub that grows wild in the Mediterranean. They are picked then pickled in brine. Used as a condiment, they add a distinct piquancy.

Cheeses — We use several Italian cheeses and French chevres (goat cheeses) in this book.

Chevres range from soft to firm and from mild to strong in flavor. Boucheron and Montrachet are good choices for the goat cheese novice as they are mellow in flavor. There are also a few marinated chevres to choose from. Our favorite is Les Provençales. Marinated in olive oil and herbs, it pairs well with pasta and is superb crumbled over a salad. We have also used feta cheese, a traditional goat cheese from Greece. Feta is generally quite salty with a strong yet pleasant flavor.

The Italian cheeses used are:

Fontina — This cheese gets its name from the village of Fontin in the Italian Alps. Made from whole cow's milk, it is a soft, pale, dry salted cheese. It makes an excellent table cheese, yet it is quite good for cooking.

Fontinella — A sharp Italian cheese with a rather soft creamy texture that is well suited for pesto and risottos.

Locatelli — A hard Romano cheese made of sheep's milk. It has a low-fat content and a sharp, distinctive flavor that makes it an exceptional table cheese.

Mascarpone — Citric acid is used to curdle the cream to make this wonderful cheese. It is a very rich spreading cheese with an extremely high fat content. It has a mild flavor and can be served as a table cheese as well as added to dessert recipes.

Mozzarella — This cheese should always be eaten fresh. Once mozzarella was only made from buffalo milk, but for quite some time now it has been made with cow's milk. It has a very dense consistency and is quite bland, making it very easily digested. It melts well and is used for pizza and casseroles.

Parmigiano Reggiano — Our favorite grating cheese, it originally comes from the province of Parma, hence the name. It is a low-fat hard cheese made from cow's milk with a subtle almost sweet flavor. There are many Parmesan cheeses on the market to choose from. However, the Parmigiano Reggiano is the finest available and is well worth seeking.

Couscous — A finely milled semolina wheat that takes only minutes to prepare and is a welcome change from other grains. It has long been a staple in Mediterranean cuisine.

Garlic — No kitchen is complete without fresh garlic bulbs. Powdered garlic pales in comparison. Garlic's pungent flavor is intrinsic to many dishes we love. Throughout history garlic has been thought to be beneficial to health.

Herbs — Food is transformed by the essence of herbs. Fresh herbs are essential to our cooking style and are favored over dried. Crushing the herbs between your fingers before using them releases the fragrance and flavor. The herbs we use most frequently are:

> **Basil** — An integral part of Mediterranean cuisine, basil has a sweet flavor and is very aromatic. It is a well-known companion to tomatoes as well as a major ingredient of pesto.
>
> **Bay Leaves** — It has been said that the Greeks dedicated the bay tree to the god Apollo, the god of medicine, as it was believed to increase health and happiness. Spicy and pungent, bay leaves are used to enhance soups, stews, chicken dishes and sauces.
>
> **Parsley** — The Italian flat-leaf variety is the parsley we prefer. Its leaves are flat and glossy green, and it is by far the most flavorful of all the parsleys.
>
> **Rosemary** — A versatile herb, it adds a sweet flavor to roasted chicken and an unusual accent to soups and sauces. It is believed to be useful as an aid to digestion.
>
> **Saffron** — Has been called the spice of kings and rajas, and we wholeheartedly agree. Each saffron crocus yields only three stigma threads.

It takes almost 70,000 flowers to produce one pound of the spice, so it's not difficult to see why this spice is precious and costly. You only need a pinch of saffron to release its penetrating bouquet and lovely golden color. Use in soups, sauces, chicken dishes and risottos.

Tarragon — A widely used herb best known for its use in vinegars and in fish dishes. Delicious in salad dressings, vegetable dishes or sauces.

Thyme — Aromatic and ideal for flavoring sauces, stews and stuffings. There are several varieties of thyme available:

Lemon Thyme is well suited for chicken and fish.

Oregano Thyme can be substituted for oregano in sauces.

English Thyme is the most common and is delightful added to tomato sauces or in a white clam sauce.

Mushrooms — The mushroom family has made a grand appearance in the marketplace. We are all familiar with the common white domestic mushroom, which is wonderful in its own right. But there are several cultivated and wild varieties we would like to mention:

Crimini or Italian Brown Mushroom — Similar in appearance and flavor to the domestic white mushroom, this relative is usually a little larger with a light brown cap.

Enoki — Once imported only from Japan, it is

now cultivated in the United States. This delicate, long thin mushroom can be eaten raw or cooked for a minute or two.

Oyster — Ruffled soft mushroom with a mild flavor and texture. It is best eaten raw in a salad or briefly cooked.

Morels — Long conical shriveled mushroom, ranging from tan to very dark brown. This earthy mushroom has long been prized for its delicious flavor. They can be found fresh but more often dried.

Porcini or Cepes — The Italians call them *porcini* and the French refer to them as *cepes*. It is very difficult to find them fresh in this country, but the dried are excellent because the drying intensifies their flavor. They have a strong woodsy scent that can transform the most common fare into a meal extraordinaire.

Portobello — Don't be fooled by the looks of this mushroom. Large and questionable in appearance, it is one of the most flavorful mushrooms of all. It is wonderful grilled and imparts a rich meaty flavor and texture.

Shiitake, Black Forest, or Golden Oak Mushroom — Another Japanese mushroom that is being cultivated in the United States. They can be purchased fresh or dried. They have a unique flavor and texture which allows for great versatility.

Olive Oil — There are major classifications of olive oil. We use only two as we feel they are superior in quality and flavor.

Extra-virgin olive oil comes from the first pressing. It is dark green with the strong fruity taste of olives. It is best used on salads, dressings and in marinades.

Virgin olive oil comes from the second pressing. Lighter in color and flavor, it is excellent for all the above uses and also wonderful for cooking and frying.

Olivada — A highly concentrated paste made from Ligurian olives. Great as an appetizer spread on toasted Crostini or crackers. Used sparingly, olivada lends a unique flavor to many foods.

Olives — An important flavor enhancer. Here's a list of some of our favorites.

>   **Alfonso** — A delicious large, dark olive.
>
>   **Calabrese** — Khaki-colored, small dull olive. Usually packed with hot pepper, garlic and herbs.
>
>   **California Green** — Slightly dry, big meaty olive with or without pits.
>
>   **Gaeta** — Small, smooth Italian olive. Meaty with an excellent medium-bitter flavor.
>
>   **Greek Black** — Brine-cured, pungent and meaty olive.
>
>   **Italian Green** — Similar to the California green, it has more oil content which gives it a different flavor.
>
>   **Kalamata** — Considered by many to be the best of all olives. This famous Greek olive is identified by its point on the bottom. It has a perfect flavor . . . not too strong, not too salty.

Ligurian — A northern Italian small, bitter, full-flavored olive.

Moroccan oil cured — Salty, black, shrivelled olive packed in oil.

Naftalian — A middle-size mild olive.

Niçoise — Tender, tiny French black olive. It is cured in brine and herbs and then packed in oil.

Nyons — Reddish brown, small round oil-cured olive with an exceptional flavor.

Picholine — Green French delicate-flavored olive.

Royal or Victoria — A large, very delicious, black Greek olive that is cured in oil.

Sicilian — Dark spicy small olive cured in brine.

Sicilian oil cured — Same as the Sicilian but cured in oil rather than brine.

Speckled green — California small speckled with brown. Low salt with a smooth mild flavor.

Wine-cured — Large purple-black olives from Peru and Spain. They are meaty with a distinctive sharp flavor.

Pasta — There is an endless variety of pasta on the market. Although nothing can quite compare to homemade, there are several fresh pastas available as well as superior quality dried pasta. The most important thing to remember when cooking pasta is that it should never be overcooked. Tender yet firm . . . al dente!

Peppers — We have used quite a few pepper varieties in this book. The red Italian sweet, the orange semi-hot Karlo, the yellow hot wax, the plump red, green and yellow bells and last but not least, the small dried hot cayenne and cherry peppers.

When using peppers, especially the hot varieties, use only the flesh, discarding the seeds and stems. To avoid finding out that you've made it too hot, start with a small amount of hot pepper and add more only after allowing some cooking time. We prefer that they don't overpower the flavor of the dish. You can use hot pepper flakes, found in jars in the market, in place of fresh hot peppers. Both fresh hot peppers or pepper flakes must be refrigerated if you plan on keeping them for any length of time as they lose their heat if left at room temperature.

Peppercorns — We recommend a good pepper mill, as there is really no substitute for fresh ground pepper. There are black, green, brown, pink and white peppercorns. Our suggestion for an all-around seasoning is a blend of all of the above and the Tellicherry peppercorns.

Phyllo — A paper-thin pastry dough that is very versatile. It makes a flaky crust that can be used in appetizers, entrées and sweet pastries. May be purchased fresh or frozen and is readily available at most markets.

Rice — Arborio rice is the classic rice from Italy that is used for risotto. Cook Arborio rice in a heavy bottom pot for the best results.

Shallots — Shallots have a distinctive but delicate flavor, a cross between that of garlic and onion, yet more subtle.

Vegetable and Salad Greens — There is now such variety when it comes to salad greens. As gardeners, we have grown all those listed below. They are a delight to grow, but if you don't garden, don't despair. They are increasingly available in markets throughout the country. We encourage you to try them all. The various tastes, colors and textures delight the palate as well as the eye.

Arugula or Rocket — Arugula has an intense, peppery flavor. It can be enjoyed in mixed salads or as a green in soups, and it is delightful added to sandwiches.

Escarole — Can be used as a salad green combined with other lettuces, sautéed with fresh garlic and olive oil or added to soups and stews. It has a strong flavor that can stand up well to cooking.

Fennel or Finocchio — Has a light, licorice flavor and a refreshing crisp texture. One of our favorite ways of enjoying fennel is cutting the bulb into slivers and dipping it into some seasoned olive oil. It is also delicious sautéed. The feathery tops can be used to flavor sauces, fish or chicken.

Mache, Field Lettuce or Lamb's Tongue — A member of the chicory family, it grows wild in the fields of Europe in the spring. It has small oval leaves and grows in a rosette shape which can be left whole in salads. The flavor is mild and flowery. A perfect complement to arugula and radicchio.

Nasturtium Flowers and Leaves — Both the flower and leaves of this lovely plant are edible. They have a peppery flavor that adds excitement to salads or sandwiches. The flower makes a lovely garnish as well.

Radicchio — A beautiful salad vegetable of Italian origin. It is a member of the chicory family. There are two types of radicchio, but we are most familiar with the round variety. The other is called Radicchio di Treviso. It has an elongated shape more like its cousin Belgian Endive. They both have the same lovely color, variations of magenta and pink with white speckles. It makes a lovely garnish and is excellent in mixed salads or sautéed in various dishes.

Sorrel — A perennial green which is very popular in Europe. It has a lovely citrus flavor and is rich in vitamin C. Use sparingly in salads (mostly as an accent) but generously in soups and sauces.

Vinegars — Good quality vinegar has a pleasing aroma, never strong or overbearing. We use mostly red wine vinegar or balsamic vinegar in our salads and cooking.

Balsamic Vinegar — Balsamic is deep reddish brown in color and its sweet-sour full-bodied flavor animates salads, fruits and vegetables. It is of Italian origin, where it has been made for centuries. The process for making this vinegar takes many years. The wine grapes are allowed to ferment in a barrel.

When it has evaporated and the liquid is reduced, it is placed in a smaller wooden barrel. This process continues until not much of the liquid is left. The end product is this wonderful, unusual, precious vinegar.

Wine Vinegar — Made from fermenting wine grapes. The wine is allowed to ferment until it becomes acidic, which is essentially the process for making vinegar in general.

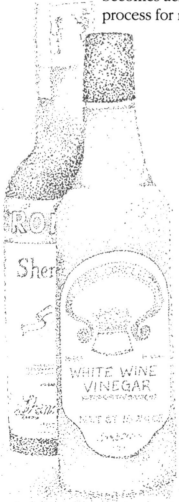

Index